Crossing the gain line

Achieving your goals in the modern world

Chapter Outline

Prologue

Genesis of 'crossing the gain line'

This book was originally intended to explain how it was possible to work twelve hour days as an editor and yet still stay physically fit, run a photography business, write two books, and start two companies without losing sleep or abandoning all hope of a social life. As the fingers began to flow over the keyboard it soon became apparent that this was made possible through a lifetime of experience and, more importantly, a rational and *simplifying* philosophy.

Rather than writing a step-by-step instruction manual, the book instead evolved to take the form of a series of philosophical rationalisations that derived from the lessons in life that we all receive, as well as the teachings of some of the greatest philosophers of the preceding centuries. It is often said that there is *'nothing new under the sun'*, and that, in all our efforts, we merely stand on the shoulders of the giants who precede us. This cannot be denied, and this book has certainly been influenced by many of the great minds of the river of time whose words and deeds have long outlived their originators. However, I hope that this work will be perceived to be more than a mere synthesis of the ideas and wisdoms that foreshadowed it.

If there is anything useful to be derived from this book, it is the importance of philosophy as a moral and mental compass by which we may navigate the complexities of our modern existence and, if there is anything to be gained from reading it, it is the recovery of your time and the motivation to do something meaningful with it.

I can only hope that the experience of reading this book will be as profound as that of writing it.

This book is dedicated to Prince Stephie Pahlavi Zan and Professor Oliver Sacks, two personal acquaintances whose deeds have demonstrated that unconditional love and humility are the keys to the door of humanity.

Chapter One

The philosophy of self-improvement

The school of ancient wisdom, from Aristotle to Zeno[1], has tended to focus upon the way in which we view ourselves within the context of the natural world and society. Many philosophers reasoned that we are, in reality, no more powerful or significant than a small vessel sailing across unpredictable and often turbulent seas. However, such *'antiquated'* schools of thought have since given way to Western ideas of the primacy of the self, and the role of the individual as the instigator of great change and accomplishments which propel society forward - irrespective of the ensuing consequences or any scrutiny of the rationale for such advances. Of course the forefathers of both Western and Eastern philosophies lived in a far less populous and technologically more primitive age, one in which 'wisdom' served as a 'mental compass' to guide the moral direction and decisions of both societies and the individual. In the ancient world of the Buddha and Confucius, seeking a balance in life and with nature was considered to be of primary importance, an emphasis that is far removed from the calling of the modern materialistic world in which we live.

To this end, the modern Western cult(ure) of the individual creates its own gods, much as the ancient Greeks and Romans did in their time, elevating the exceptional from every walk of life to the status of icons for veneration. Whether you consider the kingdoms of business and science, or those of fashion and Hollywood, we are encouraged to revere the image and status of a few select individuals, even though today this might be in the form of a flattering portrayal by the media through film or magazine rather than idealised representations in the form of statues and mythical tales. The Romans even elevated their emperors to the status of gods upon their passing, and Greek heroes such as Heracles and Theseus eventually joined the gods as a reward for their storied feats and divine interventions. Similarly, in our contemporary

---

[1] founder of the Greek school of Stoicism (*circa* 334 – 262 BC).

Western world, the 'cult of the individual' holds us enthralled, and we appear to deify the brightest, the best, and the most beautiful, with the modern media spreading the gospel of their fame through its myriad forms. The diet, lifestyle and romantic trysts of our leading actors, academics, models, leaders and entrepreneurs are followed with a degree of detail and diligence that was not even afforded to the heroes of ancient Troy.

The reality though is that we are all born individuals; each and every one of us remarkable and deficient in our own right; each of us capable of great feats, yet prone to human failings. Some of us may rise above the 'ordinary' for a time and become regarded as leading lights within our respective walks of life, whether through good fortune, or via dedication and perseverance. However, the truth is that no one individual rises above all others based solely upon their own merits, or without influential foundations and teachings. Every great academic builds their ideas upon the foundations created by the ideas of others. Even the much vaunted Albert Einstein produced his *'annus mirabilis'* [2] while working as an examiner at the Patent Office in Bern, Switzerland, an office in which he would have had direct access to many unpublished ideas of great scientific value. Today, every modern Nobel Prize-winning scientist has a team of bright young minds working diligently under them, and even such innovative minds as those of Nicolas Tesla, Elon Musk and James Dyson have had access to many brilliant young physicists and engineers within their laboratories. This is not to seek to demean their genius or undermine their worth to society, but rather to frame everything within the perspective that very few individuals achieve great things totally unaided, even if they come to receive all the accolades.

This modern trend towards selecting the 'MVP', or 'most valuable player', from a team of talented contributors is not of course restricted to the field of science. The much vaunted artist, Damian Hirst, owns a studio which is populated by aspiring young creatives; and every star athlete has a team of managers, coaches, physiotherapists, sports nutritionists and, of course, fans who help to drive their ascent to the summit of physical accomplishment. Lewis Hamilton may have won the Formula One motor racing championship, but his success is

---

[2] From the Latin phrase meaning a 'miraculous year'

underpinned by the tireless efforts of dozens of engineers, designers, investors, technicians and supporting pit crew. These famous people are mentioned merely to illustrate the principle that stardom, celebrity and 'success' are not the culmination of one individual's selfless exploits, but rather the inevitable outcome of a human pyramid in which the many support the ascent of a fortunate few. It is possibly germane to suggest that most of us are unlikely, even if we possess the necessary talent and virtues, to find ourselves in a position in which we are privileged to rise to being the 'one' who is marked for greatness. For every thousand actors who are busy striving for recognition, there is only one Hollywood star, and for every thousand young girls striding the catwalk there can only be one supermodel.

'We are all ready to win, just as we are born knowing only life.' - Han

Even if we harbour the necessary potential, most of us will never realise the funding, the backing, or indeed the opportunity to rise to become *'primus inter pares'*, or *'first amongst equals'*. This is not to seek to discourage others from trying, or to discourage you from the pursuit of your dreams, and certainly it is not the goal of this book to dissuade anyone from engaging in the continuous improvement of self that comes from striving to achieve goals. In fact, *it is the very essence of this book.* The objective of these opening paragraphs is solely to prepare the ground for what follows – a practical and philosophical approach to self-improvement and self-fulfilment - one which is unburdened by the expectations of material reward or popular 'success'.

It could be reasoned that our primary objective should be to seek balance, or 'harmony', across the many aspects of our lives. Given our great potential as human beings, these aspects, or dimensions, span the professional, the personal, the social, the romantic, the intellectual, and the physical. To achieve balance and health, harmony and happiness, we must address all of these elements within our lives, and not be tempted to sacrifice this balance simply to achieve 'success' within any solitary domain of life's 'hexagon'. If balance is truly our goal, then we cannot hope to succeed alone. Accordingly, we must trade our time freely in order to build trust with others in our quest to attain a harmonious balance.

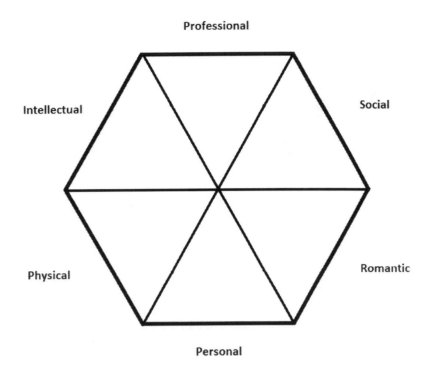

We could invoke the idea of a 'lost age of wisdom', given that we have long since lost our connection to the natural world of the ancient 'human', having ushered in a new technological and material era. There is of course little doubt that a series of technological revolutions have transformed our lives dramatically in terms of the provision of energy, healthcare, information and travel, to an extent that would certainly have been beyond the wildest imagination of those who lived only a few centuries ago. However, the technological revolution also promised us a future filled with leisure, as machines and computers dispensed with our daily drudgery and took over our repetitive tasks. Yet, despite the exponential advancement of technology, we have come to witness a culture that is dominated by ever longer working hours, a congested and despoiled landscape, and the invasion of our personal space and private lives by mobile phones and cameras. The modern factory and office demand highly skilled operations which are now increasingly performed by automated systems and computers rather than by highly paid specialists; while those more repetitive tasks, such as cleaning, call centres, and data entry, are performed by unskilled labour in those instances where it is still cheaper than automated solutions. A society based upon consumption has driven the growth of an economy that is centred upon commodities and services, whilst skilled artisans and those working the land have been greatly reduced in their range and number.

Given the fact that many of us spend most of our time running through our daily routines simply to maintain a modest *status quo*, rising early and working late into the evening in order to cover our student loans, mortgages, rent, energy bills, travel, food, and the latest digital technologies, we seldom find the time to pause to take a breath and ask *why*? Surely there must be more to life than continuing in the hope that our efforts will be ultimately be recognized and rewarded with a greater social standing and salary? The answer to this rhetorical question is of course that there is much more to life. However, the first step towards perceiving this 'reality' is to change the *distorted lens* through which we view ourselves and the modern world. Indeed, this *'pole shift'* in perspective must occur *before* we can seek to improve the *quality* of our lives. To achieve our new goal of balance and harmony, we must become the drivers of change within our lives, rather than merely being increasingly *driven* to improve the *quantity of our time* and of our 'product' that we dedicate to the constructs of our society.

This book will discuss precisely *how* we can achieve this, and *why* we should alter our *'value system'* to redirect our precious time and energies from seeking to acquire more influence, more 'power' and more material possessions to creating more health, balance and happiness within our lives.

Please do not be alarmed. There is no requirement for an advanced understanding of philosophy, no necessity to struggle with complex theories, and no need to make sudden or dramatic changes in your daily life. The goal of this book is to reflect upon our core values, and through doing so refine our decision-making processes via a series of simple and reasoned adjustments to save time and redirect our energies more gainfully.

Chapter Two

How the modern world leaves us in its wake

Modern life is a game of *'catch up'*. Indeed, most of us find that we are already behind before we have even embarked upon our journey through life. It should be remembered that we are born without any substantial records, any formal education, or debt – we enter this world with a clean slate upon which the values of our social system may be freshly inscribed.

Two of the primary teachings which are keenly etched upon our formative minds, are those of communication and co-ordination. We have to rise at an appointed hour, and follow the directions of our parents, peers and educators to a rhythmic schedule which precludes almost all activities that are not otherwise prescribed or approved. We are taught to count and talk before we even enter school, and our rate of development is earnestly compared to that of the offspring of other parents, as we are thrust unwittingly into the innately competitive social constructs of the Western world. How quickly we grow, and how soon we able to walk or utter our first words of coherent speech are all parameters which are gamely discussed by a generation of new parents, whose value systems are deeply imprinted with the mantra of competition and 'eugenic fitness'.

Perhaps the first social problem we encounter in life is that none of us are born equal. Some children are born into homes with affluent, loving, caring parents, who ensure that the needs of their offspring receive every possible attention and nurture. Others are not so fortunate in terms of provision or affection, even if their genetic deck is otherwise 'packed with aces'. In contrast to the eugenic ideologies of many civilizations, most individuals are not good at everything and, even if they were gifted academically, aesthetically and athletically, no single individual has the time, energy or resources to maximise their potential within all fields of human endeavour. According to the 'ten thousand hour' rule[3], which is now widely accepted by many thinkers, it is believed to take this period of time to master any given discipline or subject, whether this be acquiring a foreign language, learning a musical instrument, or becoming an expert in law, science, or indeed any other professional vocation. If we work or practice fifty hours a week, then it would take an individual two hundred weeks, or four years to truly master any skill. There is simply not enough time to become good at everything.

Given that, as part of our daily routine, we typically sleep for some eight hours a night - frequently fewer - spend at least an hour a day in the bathroom, sacrifice two more commuting to and from our daily ports of call, a minimum of two hours preparing and eating meals and beverages, and at least an hour on such seemingly unavoidable chores as answering unwanted calls, Emails and other daily tedium, finding these ten thousand hours to master a new skill set suddenly appears to be a daunting obstacle. After attending to the *maintenance activities* listed above (and there are of course countless others such as shopping, laundry and cleaning), we are already reduced to an allocation of only ten hours a day to devote to our daily lives, which, for a great many of us, is consumed by what we do for a living.

Simple logic informs us that it would take a thousand days, or four years *(if we took no weekends and only two weeks of vacation a year)*, to become a master at what we do for a living, and many more besides if the skill set we desire to acquire is restricted to evenings and weekends. There are two important realizations to take on board from this simple calculation. The first is that, if we want to alter the course of our lives, nothing is going to change unless we clear out the 'clutter' from our daily routine, and second, that we should fundamentally alter our view of time and start to look at time in terms of *quality* rather than *quantity*.

It is perhaps not altogether unsurprising that most of us find it all but impossible to move forward with our goals and dreams, whether this be to achieve a balance in our personal lives, to start a business of our own, or even to take up a new passion or hobby. *The positive perspective offered by this book is that we can regain a mastery of our lives and ambitions.* This can be achieved if we simplify the way in which we perceive our world and our place within it,

---

[3] Please read 'Outliers' by Malcolm Gladwell for a detailed discussion of the 'ten thousand hour' rule.

and take on board some straightforward philosophies and steps which will empower us to cross the 'gain line' towards self-fulfilment and achieve our own personal version of happiness.

Many individuals eventually develop a simplifying set of philosophies which tend to make their lives easier and more manageable (and consequently less stressful). However, not all of us do, and many of us wish that these revelations had been explained to us earlier in life so that we did not waste so many precious years of time. This is another reason why this book has been written - to save as many people as possible countless years of fruitless existence. These simplifying philosophies will be discussed in greater detail within the coming chapters, together with examples of their everyday practical applications. However, for the time being, we shall introduce them at a conceptual level so that they are ready for a more detailed consideration later within the book.

Seek a simple balance

For us to attain personal happiness and fulfilment, it is of fundamental importance that we seek to achieve balance across the many aspects, or 'dimensions' of our lives. These include the professional *(as we all have to make a living)*; the personal *(our need to read, reflect and meditate)*; the social *(for we are nothing without our collective humanity)*; the romantic *(as all souls crave intimacy and companionship)*; the intellectual *(we have to sharpen the tools of our mind)*; and the physical *(as we have to maintain a healthy body if we are to function effectively)*.

Stay focused on your priorities

Draw a simple cross upon a piece of paper [4]. This effectively divides the paper into four quarters, or quadrants. In the *top-left quadrant* list those things you **have to get done** today. In the *top-right quadrant* list those **key objectives** that you would like to get done to move yourself forward in your desired direction. In the *bottom-left quadrant* itemize all those **little**

---

[4] This is an adaptation of the wisdom of the late Stephen R. Covey, 'The Seven Habits of Highly Effective People'

important tasks and chores that you can't avoid, but might be able to bundle together for a later date. In the *bottom-right quadrant* list all the **bits and pieces** on your mind which are neither important, nor particularly urgent.

This process will be discussed in greater detail later, but an illustration of this exercise may be found depicted below. A young retail manager, who we shall call Clarissa, is presently unmarried, but owns and dog and dreams one day of becoming a professional fashion photographer. Within the *top-left quadrant* she lists her inescapable priorities for the day; while in the *bottom-left quadrant* she details those important things that she will need to do soon. In the *top-right quadrant* she compartmentalizes those activities which she needs to be focusing on to transform her passion for photography into a profession and, finally, within *the lower-right quadrant* she jots down some thoughts on what she would like to do in her spare moments later that day.

Walk the dog *Call Sam* *Send minutes to Ralf* *Book service for car* *Buy groceries*	*Learn how to use Photoshop* *Research prime lenses* *Search for online marketing* *course*
Pay gas bill *Cut new door key* *Process images* *Dog food*	*Check out new movie releases* *Surf Instagram* *Shop for new T-shirts* *Share cartoon on Facebook*

Clarissa's proposed day divided into quadrants

Clearly Clarissa has to take care of her dog Albert, have something to cook for her evening meal, send the day's minutes to her line manager Ralf, ensure that she continues to be able to drive to and from work, and call her father Sam who is waiting for the results of a hospital scan to reassure him.

Now that she has emptied the thoughts and obligations from the top of her mind on to a piece of paper, she performs the following exercises to free up time and organise her tasks as efficiently as possible.

1. **Batch all repetitive activities**

Those less urgent, but nonetheless important items which were allocated to the *lower-left quadrant* need to be prioritised and compressed into bundles, or 'batches'. For instance, Clarissa needs to have a spare key cut for her visitors and stock up on dog food, but she can get these and other essentials done when she visits the local shopping mall on Saturday afternoon on her way back from work. As for processing the iPhone images from last weekend's high school reunion, this can be done more efficiently when she has more to do and learns how to make her images look even better with Photoshop image processing software. As for the gas bill, this can be paid along with all the other bills in one go at the end of the month. By means of this simple filter, time can be liberated for more gainful activities simply by the process of *batching* such minor tasks. This is a simple application of the notion that efficiencies are gained when you do not alternate between tasks or locations in any one period of time.

2. 'En passant'

Another important principle is that of *'en passant'*, which is French for *'while passing'*. This simply translates as doing important things as the opportunity arises, rather than going out of your way to do them. In practice, this means stopping as you pass by the Post Office to post a letter and buy a book of stamps, or picking up spare cash when you come across a branch of your bank or an ATM, rather than waiting until the hour of urgent need and having to make a detour and stand in line, thereby wasting valuable time. Consider how many valuable hours you could save every week just by cooking four portions and storing three, or making only one major expedition to the supermarket rather than countless small trips to the local corner store *(or by having online groceries delivered)*. This elementary principle is highly transformative, as it liberates many hours of precious time and energy for more gainful activities.

3. Unclutter your routine

As for the *lower-right quadrant*, this is simply filled with idle distractions which are of little use or benefit. Such *'displacement activities'* should simply have a line drawn through them. This process of uncluttering your life should extend to all aspects of your world and daily routine, from buying unnecessary additional cookware for 'special events', to refraining from the temptation to fill your wardrobe with garments for all conceivable occasions, and avoiding the impulse to buy some more garden furniture in case next summer's barbeque is a popular hit. Wasting precious time and resources in an effort to cover all eventualities is not a blueprint for happiness, nor is it a path towards a more rewarding and productive life.

The same principle applies to your life *'online'*. *Do you really need a thousand contacts distributed across half a dozen social media sites? Are all of these contacts going to turn out to be considerate friends, resilient allies, or helpful professional acquaintances?* It would seem unlikely.

Will you really have time to make it to all of their events or to sift through all their posts and various 'opportunities'? Well, only if you really want to be trapped in the mire of the bottom-right quadrant. Not so very long ago, before the advent of Facebook and Linked-in, one had to rely upon introductions from trusted friends and colleagues to expand one's social circle. In this digital age, the flood gates into one's personal privacy and peace of mind can be opened merely by a momentary, thoughtless click or careless finger...

We will discuss this key concept in more detail later in the book, but please bear in mind that it is of paramount importance, within all of our actions, activities and affairs, that we remember that **less is more**...

Crossing the gain line

As you may already have guessed, we have been progressively working our way towards the all-important *upper right quadrant*. Now that Clarissa has identified her **key maintenance activities** for the day in the *upper left quadrant*; set aside the *less urgent activities* for **batching** within the *lower left quadrant*; and drawn a line through the superfluous activities of the *lower right quadrant*, she is now free - after her working day has concluded - to set aside a block of time in which to develop new plans, skills and activities, as detailed within the upper right quadrant, and to **cross the gain line** for the day.

As we have discussed previously, most of our limited time and energy is spent merely in maintaining our *status quo* or, in other words, we expend the greater part of our days engaged in repetitive **maintenance activities** which keep us exactly where we are and prevent us from moving forward with our valuable lives. Spending as much time as possible every day within this *upper right quadrant* is absolutely essential if we are to achieve our life goals and find balance and happiness.

Life, like nature, is essentially cyclical, and our rhythmic patterns of sleeping, eating, resting and grooming cannot be neglected for long without a loss of vitality or in our ability to function socially. Thus a certain number of hours each day have to be dedicated to meeting and greeting, chores, sleep and the maintenance of the self. This however does not mean *that such maintenance activities cannot be productive, and can even be cultivated to become pleasurable...*

'Sleep is the best meditation,' The Dalai Lama

Sleep is not only a pleasurable elixir to a tired mind, it also serves as a tonic for new ideas. Indeed, we put the computational power of our subconscious mind to good use when we go to bed with a head full of questions and information, and allow our brains to process the information overnight. It is amazing how we can often retire to bed conflicted and confused, and yet wake up refreshed with a clear mind and a clear decision. The importance of sleep in the processing of memories, information and ideation (dreaming) is a fascinating realm of neuroscience and one that is perhaps best studied from more scholarly tomes[5,6], but it is frequently the case that cutting edge neuroscience serves to validate ancient wisdoms, such as the old adage that it is best to *'sleep on'* difficult decisions.[7]

The evening rituals of eating and drinking may be especially beneficial to one's social or romantic life, as well for cultivating business relationships. Even a hot shower or a warm bath can provide an invigorating or pleasurable experience and, as discussed previously, the bath provides a suitable medium for meditative thought and ideation as the mind is relaxed and free from anxiety or distraction.

The concept of crossing the gain line is perhaps best illustrated using the sports of rugby and American Football. In both cases the ball enters active play from a resting position and has to be handed or passed backwards before any attempt at forward movement may be ventured. Enormous effort and energy is frequently expended even in getting the ball back to its original starting point and, all too often, the ball can end up going backwards until it is recaptured by the opposition. This sporting metaphor also holds true in our daily life. Each day we start afresh and seek, through individual effort or team work, to get the 'ball' into motion and carry it further forward than it was the day before. Often we have frustrating weeks in which we seem to make no forward progress, and additional effort is regularly required to devise new strategies, or 'plays', to get the ball moving forward once again. All of the effort that we expend in restarting the day and getting the ball back to its original starting position after the ritual cycle of sleep, commuting, team meetings, and answering all of those obligatory Emails is a necessary part of the recycling of the ball, and it is often not until the later part of the day, or even the evening, that we finally get the chance to cross the gain line and move forward with our objectives.

---

[5] Human Sleep and Cognition, Gerard A. Kerkhof and Hans P. A. van Dongen, 2010
[6] Sleep and Dreaming: Scientific Advances and Reconsiderations, Edward F. Pace-Schott, 2003
[7] Old adage 'sleep on it' is true. https://www.sciencedaily.com/releases/2012/10/121012074741.htm

The quality paradigm – 'less is more'

The golden rule of quality rather than quantity applies to all aspects of our lives, from the office to our hours of recreation. Positive gains and outcomes are best achieved through focus, technique and efficiency, rather than from grim determination and persistence. Bear in mind that one popular definition of insanity is, *'repeating the same mistake over and over again and expecting a different outcome.'* In the spirit of preserving our productivity (as well as our sanity), much of what we do is inherently experimental, from testing new ideas to trying out new fashions and technologies. Good ideas tend to be adopted as old ways become outmoded, while bad ideas are usually quickly abandoned. We cannot avoid making mistakes as individuals or as a society, but when we do make them and survive to become wiser, then we should not repeat them if at all possible...

Making the most of every moment

It is truly amazing what the prepared and focused mind can achieve within a very short period of time. A skilled typist can maintain a speed of 150 words per minute for up to an hour (that's 9,000 words); a helicopter crew can scramble from their rest towards an airborne rescue in a few minutes; and the Rubic's cube puzzle has been solved in under ten seconds on countless occasions. Just imagine what your mind, when motivated and focused, can achieve in an hour. You could learn to use a new software package, compile a new résumé, or write and memorize a short speech to make a critical impression on a client or manager.

'One cannot actualize one's goals until one visualizes them clearly in the mind's eye.'

Mike Mentzer [8]

---

[8] A famous bodybuilder and philosopher who was born in 1951 and died in 2001.

However, before you plan to do anything, follow the **IVE** mantra. This stands for **Ideation, Visualization** and **Execution.**

First, within a relaxed state of mind on a couch, on a train, or in a bath, allow your subconscious mind to imagine your desired goals. This process is called **ideation** and is key to the planning process. *Ideation* is defined as the process of forming ideas or images. In practice the subconscious mind is far better than your working conscious mind at many tasks, and the bewildering processing power and speed of the subconscious 'supercomputer' is discussed in fascinating detail by other authors.[9]

Second, it is necessary to **visualize** what you want to achieve and how you are going to do it. Be specific – it is important to picture within your mind exactly what the end goal is, including where you will be, what milestones you will achieve along the way, what you will be able to do or have accomplished, what obstacles you will likely have to overcome, and which skills or resources you will need to acquire to make this vision possible. *What we programme our subconscious minds to do today becomes tomorrow's reality.*

For the purposes of practical illustration, let us return to the case of Clarissa, a young store manager who works within the retail fashion industry. She was drawn to fashion from an early age and, despite gaining entry to her preferred industry, Clarissa has become far from content with her daily routine. Since graduating from college with a degree in accountancy, her daily routine is dominated by the analysis of endless sales figures, in addition to which she has to file daily reports and publish the weekly shop staff rotas and attend interminable meetings. She has become bored with the routine and *ideates* that, in order to rekindle the spark in her life, she desires to become a professional photographer and produce some of the beautiful images she sees every day. She *visualizes* taking fashion images for her company and spending more time with designers and models, with a long-term view of a move into the company's international marketing department which will afford extensive travel and photographic opportunities.

---

[9] Read 'Blink' by Malcolm Gladwell

To make this dream a reality, Clarissa assembles her plan of action into a set of key steps with a *specific* **objective**, a *defined* **action** and the **necessary steps** that are required in order to achieve the *specified goal*.

Objective	Action	Necessary steps
Upgrade from iPhone to a professional camera	Buy camera with annual bonus	1. Research prices & capabilities 2. Look at feedback and customer reviews 3. Look out for discounted equipment or end of stock
Attain professional level of photography	Take courses and join fashion photography group	1. Join fashion photography group on MeetUp 2. Seek professional for weekend lessons 3. Attend a minimum of 50 shoots over next twelve months 4. Sign up for nofilmschool.com
Build professional fashion network	Network actively with fashion professionals	1. Invite head of marketing department for a coffee to discuss ideas. 2. Attend MeetUp socials 3. Contribute actively to Facebook fashion groups 4. Organise charity fashion show
Build reputation as a photographer	Create personal brand name	1. Have business cards designed 2. Set up photography website 3. Use Instagram & Flickr to promote images & 'brand' 4. Create fashion blog

Finally, Clarissa needs to set her plans into motion. She must **execute**. For each objective she estimates the number of hours that are required to move the plan forward. She then adds to Google Calendar which actions she will undertake on which specific days.

We will revisit the mantra of **IVE** again later, but for now it is important to grasp that is only through the formative process of planning, focusing and executing with a clear vision that can we realistically hope to make lasting or gainful changes to our lives. If our thinking is cloudy then the expected outcomes will not be clear.

Take a moment to think...

There are a few more important principles that need to be grasped before we can begin to enjoy a more relaxing and harmonious life. One of these is the importance of the precious and crucial moment that arises between an event and our response to it. Sometimes we simply have no alternative but to react quickly to an event or situation, as we have no time to think or reflect on the best possible response and the likely outcomes. Those who have the ability to think quickly on their feet certainly have an advantage, but in most cases we do have the opportunity to pause for reflection or to delay a critical decision. If you cannot request a day to consider or mull over an important decision, then seek to delay the inevitable response with a series of questions. Avoid instinctive reactions when provoked, and always adopt a neutral or passive response to those who seek to bait or antagonize you. Most conflicts tend to arise from misunderstandings, but whether they occur through accident or design, they are almost always a waste of energy, if not entirely counterproductive. Always remember what peace and productivity may come from a diplomatic response or a muted silence.

Leave carpentry to the carpenter

Last, but not least, leave specialised tasks to the experts. You wouldn't normally design your own computer chip or perform complex surgery on an injured wrist, so why insist on trying to repair your own car or dishwasher? It is fundamentally irrational, no matter how noble your intentions. Yes, it may seem expensive to use the services of a professional rather than to allocate a Sunday afternoon to visit the parts store in a forlorn attempt to save a few hundred hard-earned pounds or dollars on a mechanic or engineer. However, in reality, you would spend far longer attempting to learn to solve the problem than it would take to call in a professional, and your own time is most productively spent doing what you do best and monetizing it. Think of it in more pragmatic terms. If a car needs to have its spark plugs cleaned or replaced then it would cost you the price of a manual, the tools required to measure the gaps and clean them, plus a set of new spark plugs - just in case - not to mention the countless hours spent under the hood and reading through the reference manual. A couple of hundred euros, pounds or dollars to park the car at a garage while you undertake a business trip would seem a more prudent and productive use of your time and money. So, unless you desire to take up carpentry as a hobby, leave it to the professionals...

Chapter Three

The importance of crossing the gain line in self-fulfilment

If we are honest with ourselves, a great many of us do not lead a full, happy and contented life. For those of you who are fortunate to do so, then this book may still be of some value, but you are not the intended audience. Most of us, whether as a consequence of our social programming, a deeply imprinted 'need' to compete with others, or simply because we elected to take *'the path of least resistance'*, have failed to find happiness and self-fulfilment. We are, so to speak, 'fish out of water', and tend to find that our daily existence serves to meet the expectations of others rather than to satisfy our own needs and desires. Such a state of affairs weighs heavily upon us, and we frequently feel listless and tired, progressing through life via a well-worn and rather repetitive routine. If this sounds all too familiar, then you are cordially invited to read on. We will begin this chapter by asking how and why we came to find ourselves in this position, and then move on to a discussion of how we can reprogram ourselves to be governed by a higher set of values and judgements. Once we have accepted that the record of our lives is stuck in a groove, we can at last seek to redirect our energies towards what makes us contented and feel fulfilled as sentient beings.

The power of social conditioning

We live in a technologically advanced and highly regulated society - one which is driven by the desire for profit, specialization, and competition. As such it is perhaps inevitable that we are pressured to perform from an early age and to become the best that we can be. The problem is that our system of social processing is highly ordered and tends to invest only limited effort in *actually assessing our individual aptitudes and interests*. Although our 'early years' education tends to be fairly unpressured, as we are gently coaxed to walk and talk, and to learn through a system of play and social engagement with our fellow pre-schoolers, parents and teachers. We are encouraged to draw and to paint, to assemble simple structures, and to browse through picture books. This is probably how we first learned to communicate as a species, as the earliest recorded writings from our civilisation were images etched into clay tablets or symbolic representations drawn on rocks and cave walls. This is unsurprising, given the primacy of our visual sense and, as small children, we actively enjoyed learning the elementary rudiments of art, engineering, computation, and language.

However, despite the promising nature of our formative educations and the seemingly inadvertent realization that this was precisely how the human brain was designed to learn and develop, the overwhelming impulse of our ruling bureaucratic elite has been to assess, sort and segregate individuals on the basis of their strongest perceived aptitude from the earliest possible age. Thus the curriculum of our educational funnel quickly narrows, as we are categorised as mathematicians, social scientists, linguists, lawyers, or engineers from an early age. For instance, in many schools and colleges, the provision of art classes is limited, and the study of the wider 'arts' is generally limited to the humanities; namely our selective version of history, a carefully 'approved' set of English literature texts, and social geography. The curriculum of preferred subjects tends to focus upon those subjects which are perceived to be of the greatest value to corporate society - specifically mathematics, economics, computing and the sciences[10]. One could of course regard this as favouring those who are born with a left hemispherical bias[11] and consequently an aptitude for logic; actively excluding those who are gifted with other intellectual traits, such as a penchant for creative design, advanced social communication skills, or abstract problem-solving skills. Such is the nature of the Western education system that many gifted individuals may never come to realize their repressed abilities, if they ever come to light at all. This is, in a sense, a human tragedy, as we are invariably at our happiest when we find ourselves within our own individual element.

Today's education system prioritises the importance of learning and of accepting the established version of thinking as 'published' by the academic elite, rather than encouraging

---

[10] All four sciences, if we include chemistry, biology, physics & geography, and exclude computer science, economics and psychology *(which could also be deemed to be sciences)*.
[11] 'Two Halves of the Brain', by Kenneth Hugdahl and Ren Westerhausen, 2010.

young people to question the established order of knowledge which is, after all, the purest manifestation of intelligence. Once we cease to challenge the foundations of knowledge, then we begin to blindly accept the structures and processes that govern our world, how it functions, and our place within it. This tacit acceptance of vested interests affects all actions and ideologies, whether we are considering religious doctrines, economic systems, or even why the internal combustion engine continues to dominate our industrial landscape.

For instance, accepting that Jesus Christ was the 'son of God' who was born into the world to save sinners is, however admirable or romantic a notion, a personal belief. Although we can reasonably argue that such a historical figure actually existed and that, from a philosophical perspective at least, that his teachings strongly resonate with Immanuel Kant's notion of the *moral imperative*[12], which states that, if we all act with the greater good in mind, then we would certainly create a happier and more harmonious society. Although this should perhaps be the subject of another book, better written by a religious scholar than a generalist, the point being made is that religion is fundamentally a 'belief system' rather than a rigorously tested set of natural laws which can be precisely defined, measured or predicted.

Equally, any statement that communism or capitalism represents the best, or indeed the only viable socioeconomic order also constitutes a belief system, rather than an indisputably proven, evidence-based conclusion. The same could be argued for the Western preference for 'democracy' and the *'democratization'* of other non-Western nations which evolved their own systems of governance over thousands of years. The fields of economics and anthropology, like those of phrenology, psychiatry and eugenics before them, are founded upon a system of collective observation and interpretation which can never be truly free from subjective judgement, bias, or indeed the selective exclusion of inconvenient facts. Again we cannot dwell on this contention, as it is not our intended path of reason, but we should recognize that our Western educational system, for all its merits, is a system of conditioning of the mind rather than an incubator of creative talent.

---

[12] A strongly-felt principle, or 'conscience', which compels us to act in a certain moral way for the common good.

'If you do what you love, you'll never work a day in your life'

It is possible that many of us will never realise our full potential, whether we could have been accomplished artists, photographers, inventors, or orators. Our schools and societies were largely disinterested in our full range of aptitudes and, in accordance with the will of our elitist culture, the vast majority of us did not attend leading academic institutions in which we were encouraged to cultivate the skill set and connections necessary to become leaders. Therefore, most of us remain unhappy for a reason that we cannot *quite seem to put our finger on…* For some it is simply because they are unable to exercise or to develop their full set of natural abilities; for others it is that they cannot identify or pursue their 'true purpose' in life, whether this be as guidance counsellors, healers, inventors, artists, or inspirational speakers. To put it another way, how many of us had an opportunity during our formal education to explore our potential to become herbalists, conservationists, pilots, navigators, architects, philosophers, or photographers? Of course, if we are not given a chance to explore our full potential, then we are unlikely to find our natural medium or to become happy in it, given that we have been conditioned to follow another path in life that lies far from our innate abilities. Of course becoming an accountant, a solicitor, a banker, or a dentist may have its material rewards and convey the illusion of security, but these fringe benefits do not necessarily encourage us to make full use of our potential as human beings or to enjoy our professional preoccupations which take up the lion's share of our day.

The bottom line, so to speak, is that we are conditioned to serve a system rather than being at liberty to become what we desire to be. As such, we compete to occupy pre-determined niches within a highly stratified society or, in other words, we serve to satisfy a prevailing demand for jobs within a highly defined and regulated labour market. One could argue that this is merely a social construct in which seemingly senseless roles are created within a system which has long since lost touch with the natural world - unless of course you prefer to view public relations, wellness coaches, literary agents, special political advisors, or spokesmodels to be essential elements of a balanced economy. Vast numbers of individuals now work within the realm of the Internet, programming virtual social networks, writing code for banks, firewalls or antivirus software, or creating platforms for accounting companies, online retailers, and media companies (amid countless other activities within the domain of the cloud server).

Most of the wealth of the Western world, measured in terms of GDP [13], derives from 'service industries', from which the financial services sector is often separated for the purposes of estimating 'social worth', and that is before we even consider other contributors to GDP such as the public sector, which includes government, health and education systems[14]. Those of us who seek to live 'closer to nature' are precluded from doing so, as all land is now owned and priced at a premium, while entering the emerging 'green sector' is, at best, difficult. Even artists and those who wish to make their fortunes elsewhere to generate the necessary wealth to 'return to the land' are obliged to court those who hold the purse strings to make a living.

A deeply instilled culture of competition

A lengthy discussion of the balance between human 'altruism' and competition is certainly beyond the scope of this book, save for acknowledging that most of us possess the capacity to be selfless, nurturing and caring members of an extended human family or 'society'. After all, only a small proportion of the population could be clinically 'classified' as psychopathic[15], and therefore lacking any sense of empathy.[16] It could be argued that even modern humans, if left to their own devices, prefer to live within extended groups or small communities. This can still be seen today in modern tribes scattered across the globe or, closer to home, within gypsy 'traveller' communities. Almost certainly this was our common level of social organisation during the Neolithic age[17] of the hunter-gatherer.

---

[13] The GDP, or Gross Domestic Product, is the monetary value assigned to all goods and services that are produced within a country's borders during a specific time period, and may include healthcare, tourism and even prostitution.
[14] For a breakdown of UK GDP per sector http://www.gov.scot/Publications/2008/12/04092147/4
[15] estimated to be less than 1% of the population. Kent A. Kiehl and Morris B. Hoffman (2014).
[16] 'The Wisdom of Psychopaths' by Kevin Dutton (2012)
[17] circa 10,200 to 2,000 BC

This makes social sense. If we share tasks across groups we can save immense amounts of time, whether in terms of foraging, childcare, cooking, farming, or communal defence, not to mention more modern activities such as shopping or setting up 'Wi-Fi' communication networks. You might of course argue, as Jared Diamond[18] has done, that the technological advancement of civilization was ultimately made possible through the industrialization of agriculture, which released an ever greater proportion of society to engage in more creative pursuits such the development of science and 'culture'. However, what we are suggesting is that small communities, or extended families, function more efficiently by sharing the responsibilities of childcare and the provision of daily needs, including such everyday activities as shopping and cooking. What we mean by 'efficiency' is the proportion of a community's time that is spent engaged in these daily maintenance activities. This 'economy of scale' contrasts with the modern trend towards the 'individualization' of society, in which solitary individuals (and single parents) forage and fend for themselves, and therefore spend a greater proportion of their day engaged in essential maintenance activities. While it could be argued that hiring a nanny to look after your children is comparable, this is simply not the case. Enlisting other members of an extended community to take it in turns to look after your children while you go out shopping or earn additional income is in practice an 'exchange of favours', whereas leaving your child at a crèche or hiring a nanny is simply an extension of the service economy.

Modern society, whether by accident or design, has created in its wake the social construct of the 'nuclear family'[19], in which members of the same closely related family are encouraged to live together within a self-contained house or flat. This creates the economic unit of the 'household', which is then classified economically in terms of its income, debt and expenditure. Costly commodities such as cookers, washing machines, and televisions are not generally shared beyond the confines of the household (even when they are not in use by its individual members), and thus precious resources are wasted by the replication of machines as well as through unused food, clothes, and electronic paraphernalia. More than this, the rising culture

---

[18] 'Guns, Germs, and Steel' by Jared Diamond (1997)
[19] 'The elementary social unit of a couple and their dependent children.'

of individualism has led to a further subdivision of the household into individual consumers, each with their own unique room, dietary requirements, wardrobe, computer, mobile phone and television. It could be convincingly argued that sharing and caring are innate human tendencies which have been lessened through our systematic abstraction away from a more natural communal way of life.

How we live is only one aspect of modern society. How we are encouraged to interact is another. The need to compete is instilled and imprinted within all levels of society from a formative age. This policy of 'Social Darwinism'[20] begins at school through competitive sports and examination grading and, by the time we reach adulthood, we find ourselves actively competing for employment, promotions, opportunities, sexual partners and much else, and thus we come to assume that this is the natural order of the world. However, in apparent direct contradiction, we are also taught the importance of the team and of teamwork. Yet, even within this advocacy of the team 'ethos', those same companies and sporting teams which promote the primacy of the team structure, engage in the process of establishing which team member is perceived to be the 'Most Valuable Player', either by popular acclaim or through an internal political process. These exalted individuals are then presented to society as icons and public role models. To the victors inevitably go the spoils and all of the privileges. So much for teamwork…

However, individual team members cannot compete against one another if the team is to be efficient and successful. Inevitably, due to the inherent contradictions arising within this duality of seeking to promote a team spirit and anoint individual stars, time, energy and focus are invariably dissipated through endless internal politics and feuding, as rival team members jostle for favour and position under their leaders, rather than collaborating to ensure that the task at hand is completed as efficiently and quickly as possible. Imagine a world in which you could go home to rest or recreate as soon as your work was done, rather than spending your office hours competing to be seen to work the longest hours and to take the shortest possible lunch break.

---

[20] Social Darwinism: Science and Myth in Anglo-American Social Thought, Robert C. Bannister, 1989.

Utopia may well be an unattainable objective, but the insanity of internal competition is a fallacy of the new world order.

The path of least resistance

As young people most of us found ourselves under pressure from our friends, families and schools to comply with 'normative' social and career expectations. It is generally anticipated, when responding to such questions as *'what do you want to do for a living?'* or *'what is your intended career?'*, that we will offer responses which are perceived to be outwardly respectable. Answering questions about your desired career path with such prestigious institutions as the 'law', 'medicine', or 'architecture' generally elicits a favourable response; while less esteemed, though no less responsible, career avenues such as 'teaching', 'nursing', and 'science' still receive social validation. However, when the response deviates from commonly held perceptions of social 'normalcy' and takes a turn towards the esoteric with such wild and untamed notions as becoming a 'herbalist', 'actor', or 'tattoo artist', then the individual may start to sense that their social standing has become a little more tenuous. If the individual's alignment remains uncorrected, such a sense of social unease can rapidly turn to feelings of exclusion or alienation, and before long the individual will either have to rethink the course of their life entirely or else find a more accommodating social clique on the fringes of society. While we can change our social affiliations relatively easily, this strategy of evasion becomes more difficult when it comes to our families or academic establishments, as such institutions tend to hold a powerful design upon our futures and are able to exert a far greater influence.

Perhaps unsurprisingly, many of us succumb to this relentless pressure, fearing exclusion from one of our most basic human requirements – the need for love, nurture and acceptance. Often we reject our heart's desire and intuition, and instead opt to take *the path of least resistance* towards conformity and 'security'. We will of course always harbour a sense of regret, but before long we find that we have ground our way through the long thankless hours and poverty of higher education and training to enter the ranks of the 'eight-to-eight' professionals, whose lives are an unrelenting routine which is occasionally punctuated by such approved distractions as office parties, society weddings, and possibly even a solitary week of honeymoon as our one brief taste of happiness.

However, this book is not intended to be about how we came to find ourselves in our present predicament. Rather than electing to remain generally dissatisfied with life, this book sets out a plan of action as to how we can change our lives for the better by 'repurposing' our efforts, developing a healthier philosophy and values, and making use of simple tools to ensure that we are more efficient and effective with our limited time. Once we have done this, then we will be able to free up the necessary time and energy to **cross the gain line** and cultivate a more rewarding and satisfying way of life.

The power of reprograming

What we have been discussing so far within this chapter, in rather general terms, is the power of social conditioning and how it affects our life decisions and personal behaviours. The centres of our midbrain which govern conditioning and reward are highly conserved within all mammals, which means that they are very old in evolutionary terms. The main centres are known as the amygdala *(which mediates fear conditioning)* and the ventral tegmental area *(which mediates reward)*. These more ancient parts of our brain, in conjunction with our higher centres of learning and decision-making, are readily conditioned through the use of fear and reward. Although the fascinating neuroscience of the mid-brain in fear and conditioning can be studied in greater detail elsewhere[21], it should be noted that human behaviour can readily be reinforced by rewards or deterred by punishment. This is, after all, the basis for many of the social constructs of our society and much of our penal system.

This so-called *'operant conditioning'*[22] through social reward or punishment of course begins at an early age. If we are good children, then we receive a reward such as a bag of sweets, a treat,

---

[21] *e.g.* 'Anxious' by Joseph E. LeDoux (2015)
[22] Operant conditioning is a form of learning in which the strength of a behaviour is modified by its consequences *(i.e. reward or punishment).*

or a school prize. If we are deemed to have been naughty, then we are punished by physical or psychological pain, such as a strike to a sensitive area or by sensory deprivation within a room that lacks such entertaining distractions as toys or video games. As we enter our teens, by which point we are deemed to be old enough to know better and to have developed a greater social 'awareness' in terms of what is considered to be right or wrong, then the rewards tend to become more profound and the punishments more extreme. A difficult adolescent may be excluded from school, or even expelled, and those participating in behaviour *perceived to be* antisocial or criminal may risk arrest or even incarceration. Approaching or upsetting members of a higher social caste in the 'wrong way' can result in alienation or even social exile, and young boys and girls quickly learn who they can and can't talk to, or formally approach, through such *aversive conditioning*[23].

By the time we are fully-fledged adults, such aversive social conditioning takes the form of police cautions, 'ASBOs'[24], restraining orders, banishment from communities, being fired from work, blacklisted from employment, and of course formal imprisonment. Those who do not violate society's great unwritten *'magna carta'*[25] of undesired behaviours may, if they please the right people, be suitably rewarded with promotions, pay rises and a multitude of other perks, including holidays, cars and desirable sexual partners. The greater the punishments and the rewards, the more powerful the conditioning.

A literally chilling demonstration of the power of social conditioning was amply illustrated in the experiments of Stephenson[26]. In this case *'fear conditioning'* was applied to show how humans *(and lower primates)* may be become averse to a certain behaviour when it is reinforced and 'policed' by other members of the community, even when no individual actively participating in administering a punishment can actually recall why the specific behaviour is neither condoned

---

[23] Associating an undesirable behaviour or action with an unpleasant shock or punishment.

[24] Anti-Social Behaviour Order - a civil order designed to protect the public from anti-social behaviour that causes, or is likely to cause, harassment, alarm or distress.

[25] Meaning 'great charter' or document, which historically contained 63 clauses detailing specific grievances relating to the misrule of King John (1215).

[26] Stephenson, G. R. (1967). Cultural acquisition of a specific learned response among rhesus monkeys. In: Starek, D., Schneider, R., and Kuhn, H. J. (eds.), Progress in Primatology, Stuttgart: Fischer, pp. 279-288.

nor tolerated[27]. In this rather sadistic experiment, five monkeys were placed in a cage with a set of stairs that led to an enticing reward, in this case a banana. If any one of the monkeys attempted to climb the stairs to take the banana, the other monkeys were sprayed with cold water as a negative conditioning stimulus. Before long, the mere act of attempting to climb the stairs triggered a frenzied attack upon the transgressing individual, a response that became so deeply engrained that, after a short period, the beatings occurred *without the need for a cold shower to reinforce the rule* or for any 'new' monkeys, who were subsequently introduced to the cage, *to ever have experienced or witnessed a cold shower.*

From this 'classical' experiment, we can see that the communal fear of a behaviour that has become a social taboo may be perpetuated and violently reinforced without any apparent rhyme or reason. We can observe this behaviour today in ritual public shaming over expense accounts or sexual behaviour that is widely 'perceived' to be deviant. Stephenson's experiment lucidly shows how social taboos are created and enforced as we, being social beings[28], fear becoming ostracised from the lifeline of our society and its opportunities. Social exclusion may of course take many forms, from being publically shunned to complete expulsion from a community. In extreme cases it can even lead to physical assault, rape or murder (*e.g.* 'honour killings'[29], gang rapes or 'stonings' for sexual associations or behaviour perceived to be inappropriate by a specific community).[30]

So it comes as no great surprise that many young people fear to stray from the path that is 'laid out' for them, and instead elect to follow the 'path of least resistance', studying and training for long hours, often well into their thirties, owing to their underlying anxiety to 'fit in' and become accepted. To this end, they will encumber themselves with enormous debts, forgo their weekend and holiday 'entitlements', and defer marriage and courtship until their period of peak fertility has long since passed.

---

[27] 'The Munchausen Complex: Socialization of Violence and Abuse,' by Richard L. Matteoli (2011)
[28] Rather than solitary animals or predators.
[29] 'Honour' Killing and Violence: Theory, Policy and Practice' edited by Aisha K. Gill, C. Strange, K. Roberts (2014)
[30] 'Sexual Politics' by Kate Millett, University of Illinois Press (2000)

Consequently, many of us find ourselves come to experience a 'crisis' as we enter the latter half of our lives, and realize that the rewards for which we sacrificed the best years of our lives are either absent or entirely underwhelming. Tired and demoralised, we take stock of our lives and may despair at the realisation that we are effectively excluded from so many of the privileges and freedoms of youth which we inadvertently sacrificed to 'get ahead'. For those of you who find yourselves in this quandary, please do not despair. There is still much that we can remain optimistic about, as there are many radical and gainful changes that may yet be introduced into our lives.

However, we must reflect upon our deeply embedded behaviours before we can start to methodically deconstruct and subsequently challenge them...

When we first begin to challenge the rationality of our social constructs, drives and behaviours, it can be a little unsettling, not least because we are questioning who we really are as individuals, and how constructively we have spent much of our lives. Our comedians ritually poke fun at our way of life and the often bizarre behaviours of human society, taking the somewhat gentler route to the subconscious mind to enable us to laugh at our absurdities without taking the subliminal truth too literally. Our lives are no laughing matter however, and our time, health and happiness are the only resources we truly possess. If the extent to which our social conditioning affects our daily lives is not immediately clear, it may serve as a useful exercise to illustrate this point with some specific examples.

Other than citing the more obvious example of conditioning a child through reward or punishment, there exist more insidious, yet no less powerful methods for the operant conditioning of adults. One of the most frequently abused is the stark choice of unemployment or of working 'professional hours'. For those who do not enjoy the protection of a powerful union and consequently find themselves floating as 'free agents' within the open labour market, the expectation that an employee will complete all their allotted tasks to the satisfaction of their line manager or employer is deeply entrenched. Given that the easiest way of 'measuring' an employee's performance at work is not in terms of quality or productivity – which can readily be attributed to an entire team or another colleague – but by simply counting the number of hours he or she spends within the workplace, the evolution of a culture of *'presenteeism'*[31] and *'workaholism'*, in which individuals feel obligated to work extreme hours should come as no surprise. Such compliant behaviour arises through the operant conditioning of employees to believe that they may expect to lose their livelihoods if they elect to work only the 'minimum' number of hours, although this form of fear conditioning is often effectively counterbalanced by the implicit expectation of a reward, such as a bonus or promotion, for working late into the night and weekends. This form of operant conditioning is made all the more potent by combining aversive conditioning (*i.e.* the fear of loss of employment) with positive reinforcement (*i.e.* an anticipated promotion and pay rise).

While this system may work well for employers, the prevailing culture of long working hours is detrimental to society, families, individuals and to the wider economy. The economic burden of maintaining a pool of unemployed or 'underemployed' labour as a deterrent to those who are averse to working long hours is usually externalized and placed upon the shoulders of the state, given that the burden of labour is spread unevenly across the workforce. Put in simpler terms, many of us are 'overemployed' and suffer the consequences of stress, poor health, inadequate socialization and strained social and family relationships; while many other are unemployed or underemployed and are unable to make ends meet. Clearly this malaise is both a social construct and ultimately self-defeating, as performance and productivity would likely be improved if employees were motivated by being allowed to leave the workplace as soon as their tasks were completed to satisfaction. Working long hours merely for the sake of doing so is more reminiscent of a Medieval torture than of a constructive social policy.

The reality is that our sense of self-worth, as individual elements within a dystopian 21st Century culture, is founded upon the perceived utility of our contribution to society. We are valued by what we do for a living, how much we earn, where we live, and what car we drive, and are entitled to no additional social standing other than that which is bestowed upon us by the prevailing class system. We are psychologically programmed to base our sense of social worth upon how hard we work as individuals and how well we do materially. Evidently this is

---

[31] "the practice of being present at a place of work for more hours than is actually required to complete the tasks allotted, which is deemed to be a manifestation of employment insecurity."

not a formula for a balanced or happy life, and we are conditioned to begin to feel a profound sense of 'guilt' and 'worthlessness' if we take an 'idle' day of rest or do not make ourselves useful to others, even if we have no paid work to do.

Another example of a deeply engrained form of conditioning, again related to our sense of self-worth, is that of *'empowerment through acquisition'*. This takes the form of substituting emotional needs, such as the need for social validation and acceptance, or a negative body image and low self-esteem, with the acquisition of material goods like clothes, cars and furnishings. This is popularly referred to as *'retail therapy'*, and is of course driven by the ceaseless stream of alluring advertisements to which are eyes are drawn. Such subliminal advertising powerfully associates material consumption with happiness, and usually presents smiling models or families who radiate health and well-being whenever they wear or consume a given product, or visit a certain costly location. There are of course no paid adverts for a walk in the public park. For those who suffer from low self-esteem, the need to recover a sense of empowerment by buying a new car or moving into a more expensive apartment, or to overcome a negative body image by acquiring more attractive clothes to hide their physical imperfections, a visit to the shopping mall with a credit card may prove irresistible.

This brings us on to the topical issue of body image, and the promotion of idealized and remarkable physiques by the wider media. Whether we are presented with images of tanned bodies at the beach, slender catwalk models, or lean athletes, we are being actively conditioned to associate desirability with the attainment of a standard of physical perfection that is simply not within the reach of most individuals. Most of us, who do not employ the services of professional makeup artists, have perfect teeth, or possess tanned, muscular physiques are made to feel somewhat 'inadequate'. Evidently a busy mother or a city worker who rises at six in the morning and toils until nine in the evening does not have the necessary time to prepare or eat six small balanced meals a day, rest adequately, or work out twice a day in between massages and beauty treatments. Many of us take up gym subscriptions in the forlorn hope that a muscular physique will emerge triumphantly from beneath a layer of fat that just needs to be 'burned off', or further damage our health and vitality by undertaking starvation diets in order to remove the soft layer of inadequacy. While this psychological conditioning may be beneficial to the revenues of the diet, fashion and fitness industries, it does little for the self-esteem of the countless millions who will never achieve such physical beauty.

While there may be many such examples of operant conditioning within our society, there is another that may be worth examining more closely. Our finely stratified and overtly eugenic society, has evolved many distinct, as well as some more opaque socioeconomic layers. Sometimes it is explicitly clear, at least where royalty is concerned, where the elite resides, and most of us know better than to trespass upon such hallowed ground or to make unsolicited approaches to members of royal families. The same could also be said in relation to well-known celebrities or descendants of financial dynasties. However, within the office environment, high school, or shopping mall, the separation of first class and second class lounges is not always so clearly demarcated. Most of us, at some point in our lives, have crossed the threshold of 'social acceptability' in making the wrong remark or gesture to someone who is considered to be of a higher social caste or rank than ourselves. This may have occurred in the form of an unwelcome gesture of familiarity, such as putting an arm of affection around the wrong individual, or something considered to be altogether more serious, such as a written or verbal confrontation with a social superior, a spurned sexual advance, or even a physical altercation. Regardless of the nature of the affront, the social 'inferior' tends to suffer the repercussions, whether these take the form of being ostracized from 'polite society', being banished from certain walks of life, or being blacklisted and 'blackballed'.

"The fault, dear Brutus, is not in our stars, but in ourselves, that we are underlings." [32]

The subtle cues which hint at another individual's social or economic status are easily overlooked. The cut of their suit, the label of their clothes, and even their body posture and grooming, are all intended to convey the idea of 'class'. However, rather than asking how we have come to be socially conditioned to kowtow to those of higher social rank than ourselves,

---

[32] William Shakespeare, 'Julius Caesar' (I, ii, 140-141).

we might perhaps ask why we should? Why are we compelled to show greater respect to those who happen to have attended a private school than a state-funded one, or automatically accept rudeness and arrogance from someone who was born into privilege? Such fear conditioning often prevents us from making friends, especially given that many individuals from such backgrounds are actually very pleasant and personable; precludes us from creating opportunities; and grants others effective licence to offload their unwanted errands and less desirable behavioural foibles upon us with impunity. Evidently we are conditioned to feel inferior, and to behave accordingly in their presence, although, in the absence of any clearly defined or widely accepted basis for such a system of social meritocracy, we are neither morally, nor technically inferior in our station. This reasoning does not however prevent most of us from even attempting to enter the exclusive doors of certain hotels, bars, beaches and restaurants, or from engaging in the simplest of social greetings with those who appear to derive from a certain social background.

Reconstructing our perspective of the world

Perhaps the most inescapable prison we create is that which lies within our own minds. Whether these psychological prison walls are created by operant or by aversive conditioning[33], they effectively constrain our independence and capacity to enjoy our lives. For instance, disparaging remarks made by a bank manager or a potential investor can deter an entrepreneur from persevering, while being constantly overlooked when party invitations are sent out can lead to social withdrawal and the avoidance of networking for fear of further rejection. Such apprehension and anxiety becomes a powerful psychological barrier to our future personal development and progression. Consequently, we have to scale these prison walls if we are to change our lives for the better and begin our journey towards a state of balance and harmony.

Networks exert a powerful and potentially positive influence upon our lives and opportunities. While there is a strong case to be made for being selective about joining new social groups or

---

[33] This occurs when a negative response, reaction or stimulus occurs in response to a given behaviour.

inviting unknown individuals into a sphere of our lives, as all human relationships introduce an element of risk, and there is an even stronger argument for keeping our various social groups apart, opportunities arise in the form of people and not material objects or websites. Always keep an open mind and don't judge others solely based upon their appearance or 'reputation'. Everyone has something to offer, whether it be connections, wisdom, confidence, ideas, capital or simply companionship. We are, first and foremost, human beings and, as such, we need companionship and affection to preserve a healthy and balanced state of mind. Other people should always come first, electronic communications second, and material needs and distractions a distant third. You can always send an Email later, or reply to a voicemail in half an hour's time, but genuine 'face time' is the only time you can effectively bond with another individual to gain their trust and confidence. Without the key to their confidence, you will be unable to unlock the door of opportunity.

Any rotten structure has to be torn down before it can be rebuilt on more secure foundations. The first stage in our reconditioning process is to rationalize why we and others behave in a certain way. Ask yourself why you were not invited to a party, were declined for a date, or were refused a loan (or other opportunity). *In the first instance, try to see it from the perspective of the other party.* This is an immensely gainful and constructive approach. It is only when we seek to understand the rationale for the behaviour of another individual that we begin to see things from their perspective and come to realise that their behaviour is rarely irrational. Other individuals can be selfish, even psychopathic, but they are rarely irrational. If we are to understand why events have taken a certain course, we must first appreciate why others behaved as they did. This process informs and constructively empowers our future decision-making and behaviour. As our success or failure in this world (and our personal lives) is largely a direct consequence of our decisions and behaviours, a healthy engagement with our problems usually leads to positive outcomes.

Frequently it is our own behaviour that requires adjustment, and often *the most important moments in our lives are those precious pauses between an event and our reaction to it.* Life, and its many potential outcomes, are often decided within that crucial delay between an event and our response to it. We can react rashly to an unwelcome physical contact in the street or a casual coarse remark – but it is better to first pause and take a moment to consider whether the consequences of an altercation really merit the sleight endured. We can react angrily and impulsively to an unfavourable decision or decide to accept it gracefully. Often it is the individual who reacts maturely and positively to a seemingly unfair judgement who rises in public stature and self-esteem. When presented with an offer that might not initially appear to be gainful, try to secure more time to make a decision by asking if you can sleep on it, or at least get back to someone in a few hours. This will provide important time for reflection in case a hidden opportunity is not initially evident.

Once we begin to look at the world and its response to us from the perspective of others *(which can initially be a painful reflective process)*, then we can then start to reconstruct our philosophical approach in such a way that it leads to more positive actions and outcomes. Philosophy should not be viewed as an odd and rather 'academic' way of looking at life - it is the very psychological lens through which we view the world and, if our lens is cloudy, then our judgement and perspective will be opaque. This will lead us to make bad and costly decisions.

Redefining our values and goals

From our reflections on the pressures of the modern office we may take the view that the culture of long working hours is rather counterproductive, at least from the perspective of anyone who is not an owner or a senior manager. We have been conditioned to view quiet periods of reflection and contemplation as idle moments, and days off work as sheer laziness. However, just as our muscles do not grow during an intense workout, requiring rest for the processes of repair and replenishment to occur, so our minds do not assimilate and process new knowledge and ideas during intense bursts of mental activity, but rather during periods of repose and quiet reflection. Are you ever at your most creative and imaginative when you are stressed, rushing around, or sleep-deprived? Do you see a clear and positive vision of the future when you are constantly distracted by chores, phone calls, screen events and messages? These are of course rhetorical questions which are intended to illustrate a point and bring us back to our core principles of **ideation, visualization**, and **execution** which were first introduced in Chapter 2.

Before we can seek a more balanced view of the world and our place within it, we must first liberate time and seek sanctuary from its endless distractions to think, reflect and meditate on our lives. We need to change our fundamental values to start to view work as a **series of actions towards a defined goal** and *not as a daily ritual* which must occupy a certain number of hours of every waking day. If we begin by establishing the objectives of any task and visualising our path towards a successful outcome through a series of rational steps then, more often than not, we will succeed and with time to spare. The 'efficiency gains' of such a radical shift in our approach to work, in terms of both time and outcome, are entirely transformative.

We can learn the merits of this principle simply by watching others in action. Next time you call an engineer to your home, someone who is paid to complete the task at hand and not according to the number of hours they take to do it, you will find that they will have normally have diagnosed the problem, repaired the fault and left everything as they found it within an hour. How many times have you spent an entire morning or afternoon at home or in the office and achieved absolutely nothing? This is simply because when we go through the motions, or decide to do something on the spur of the moment, we usually lack focus in our approach and fail to visualize our objectives and how they can be realised before actually starting out. Ideally, we would not even commence work on any complex task until we had navigated the mental maze of its resolution. For major projects this can take days and, frequently, the key solution or inspiration may only come to us during a quiet moment of reflection when we least expect it.[34]

There is a well-known challenge on a popular reality show called the 'Apprentice' in which two teams are sent out to pound the streets of London or New York to acquire a number of rare items. So eager are they to venture forth and complete this exotic shopping list, that they frequently do not consider spending a couple of hours searching online for likely sources or appointing someone to remain in the office to coordinate their efforts. As a consequence, they usually find themselves either pounding the avenues in vain or sitting anxiously in taxis as the

---

[34] Always take a pad or a smartphone with you to make notes as ideas come to you.

deadline for the task's completion draws near. A few hours of patient planning can save days of wasted effort, yet most of us simply get dressed and rush towards the front door in our haste to begin another day of work.

This principle was perhaps best illustrated by a fellow Cambridge PhD student who would frequently not be seen for days, or even weeks at a time. When he was encountered in the office, he was to be found reading furiously, but on those occasions when he did visit the laboratory to perform an actual experiment (after countless hours of thought and mental preparation), he rose early, arrived with a keen sense of purpose and worked within uncommon focus for as long as was necessary to complete the experiments he had envisioned. It may well have taken him five years to complete his PhD, but he doubtless wasted far fewer than most of his contemporaries. His life was a healthy balance of social, athletic and academic interests, and he never appeared to undertake any activity without first clearly visualizing his objectives.

Paradoxically, *less is so often more*, and it is of fundamental importance that we seek to become goal-orientated rather than work-orientated if we are to cross the gain line.

Re-evaluating our material needs

As we need to invest time at a job or in business to earn money, it could reasonably be suggested that time and money are interchangeable forms of our most precious resource which is *'time'* - just as mass and energy are two sides of the same coin in quantum physics[35]. However, unlike money, our lost time can never be replaced.

Our conditioned impulse to engage in some *'retail therapy'* when we feel a little low and need a lift could be perceived as maladaptive, or even counterproductive. Shopping for material goods and essential commodities is merely a means to an end, whether we need to buy a new dishwasher or a suit for an interview. Perhaps a more balanced way of viewing the activity of material acquisition is to **consider every purchase to be an investment**. A gainful investment is

---

[35] Einstein's theory of 'Special Relativity', otherwise expressed as $E = mc^2$

one in which the initial outlay *in terms of time or money* is outweighed by the return. For instance, imagine that buying a new iPhone to replace an obsolete device saves you two hours a day of having to be in the office and enables you to send business Emails on the move and avoid an hour a day of scheduling through its calendar and integrated business software. If your time is worth £25 an hour and the new iPhone costs £600, then the initial outlay is recovered within eight working days.

The Dalai Lama once remarked, when asked why he owned an expensive watch, that it was not the possession of things that was of importance, but rather that we should not become 'materially attached' to, or 'possessed' by them. Perhaps his ownership of such a fine piece of craftsmanship also symbolised the importance of time as being our most precious resource; emphasising that the lifetime which is afforded to us is finite, and that we should make the very most of it.

One of the more concerning aspects of the modern materialistic malaise is our tendency to borrow against the future to finance today's requirements. This seems particularly inadvisable when a credit card or loan is used to buy a new car, dress or television. All debts have to be repaid with interest, whether these take the form of personal favours, loans, missed sleep, or credit card bills. Although it may initially appear that we need to borrow money in order to make something happen - time and patience will often present alternative solutions, even if this entails an additional part-time job or moonlighting as a freelancer during the evenings and weekends.

Put people and not activities first

As Stephen R. Covey once wisely advised in his influential work the 'Seven Habits of Highly Effective People', our days and activities should revolve around other people and not tasks or material possessions. This principle seems even more pertinent today, as we are constantly passed by others who are absorbed by their mobile phones, laptops, iPads and smart watches, seemingly oblivious to their environment and fellow human beings. To further compound the problem, many also choose to wear headphones or earplugs which render them intentionally oblivious to those around them, as they attune their minds to the beat of an electronic world which is often far from constructively filtered. Other than potentially leading to grave misunderstandings or accidents, they are simply disconnecting from the human world and its myriad opportunities. In order to pursue a gainful and happy life, we should put our fellow humans first and ensure that our various tasks rearrange themselves around our daily meetings and civilised personal exchanges and not *vice versa*.

As a useful exercise, why not spend some time, after the day's activities have wound to a close, reflecting on events from the perspective of your visual memory. Replay how you spent your time and the nature of your social interactions with friends, colleagues and loved ones. How many were reduced to a tacit acknowledgement or a swiftly introduced closing remark? Then in hindsight try to infer, from their tone and body language, what they were truly seeking from you; whether it was recognition, a sense that they were valued, or the need to discuss an important matter. How did your distracted responses make them feel? Did you allay their concerns or offer them the reassurance that they were seeking, or did you turn your head back towards some other activity or preoccupation while they were still talking to you? Some of these disrupted social interactions were potentially hurtful, while others may have been perceived as dismissive, while one might well have been a lost opportunity. Do you tend to spend your weekends and evenings alone or in the company of the same small circle of friends and family? If you do, then this may well suggest that you are putting your work and activities before other people. If this is the case, then it might help to explain your social isolation or worse, indicate that you are becoming pathologically competitive.

Most conflicts with others arise through misunderstandings, miscommunications, or a failure to interact with due respect and consideration. Regardless of its cause, friction with others is a waste of both time and energy, while constructive engagement and 'true teamwork' are psychologically enriching and ultimately more rewarding. Not taking the time to listen to what your friends and colleagues are trying to say can convey the impression that you do not care about their thoughts, feelings or opinions, especially when you would rather read a computer screen or respond to an Email than give them a few moments of your valuable attention. We are all busy in the modern world, but rushing to leave the office or finish a message rather than engage with a colleague is a clear indication that their views are less important than your time.

Aberrations in our behaviour in dealing with others, such as rushing interpersonal communications, not making eye contact, or habitually appearing to be distracted, tend to result in weakened social bonding and may result a sense of alienation. Psychology aside, not finding time for social pleasantries tends to make for a less convivial environment in which to work or live. Before long our colleagues, roommates, and extended social circles start to feel that we are hard work and begin to minimize their interactions with us. In an ever decreasing circle, we are no longer extended important social invitations and our own personal 'voice' and influence steadily become diminished and, ultimately, we risk losing the warmth and respect of our colleagues. Declining to buy a round of drinks or coffees may lead to the 'emotional bank account' with our friends and colleagues quickly becoming overdrawn, as can persistently declining after work socials. Making personal judgements or remarks, disrespecting the privacy of others, not engaging in formal greeting rituals, and failing to open the door for others are all 'red flags' in terms of our relationships. These, and many other small, yet important courtesies, are all necessary to convey the impression that we value the time and feelings of others and so avoid creating an impression of arrogance or 'aloofness'. Of perhaps greater concern is that the avoidance of such social niceties may be the harbinger of a pathologically competitive personality, one which leads others to be on their guard, individuals upon whom we depend for cooperation and our own efficiency and functionality. Very soon time will seem to drag in the office and a negative atmosphere prevails due to a widespread sense of distrust and suspicion. Such a state of affairs usually culminates in a swift departure.

It is therefore of paramount importance to focus upon being friendly and on building a sense of empathic trust with others via honest and open communication and, where reasonable, offering to take a fair share of the workload rather than shirking responsibilities or delegating as much as possible to others. If you are valued by your colleagues, then this will ultimately pay dividends when you are offered a promotion or earn glowing reviews within your professional and personal networks. As the actor Kevin Spacey once poignantly stated, we only stand to gain in life by *'paying it forward'* in terms of our investment in our personal development, relationships and careers, and a good reputation is surely one of the greatest assets we can possess in life, as it is the key to many doors. However, such a good personal standing can only be derived from the positive, professional and polite treatment of others.

Other than the counterintuitive principle of putting other people first, it is also important to become as honest with ourselves as possible and to be our own harshest critics. If we accomplish this, then we find that all incoming criticisms are either tacitly accepted or else are swiftly rejected as either spurious or unwarranted. A strong personal philosophy, born of a character built upon honesty and integrity, is invariably the best psychological shield in engaging with the outside world. Delusion and self-denial may appear to be an effective defence, but these inevitably lead to errors of judgement and a failure to respond to the criticisms of others. Such criticisms, although often insensitive, serve as lighthouses which prevent us from crashing on the rocks of misfortune. Those who do not adopt such a philosophy are at risk of the psychological distress which is caused when there is a chasm between our self-image and the perceptions of others.

The importance of crossing the gain line in attaining self-fulfilment

Having addressed some of the many pitfalls of living in a complex society and the mental traps into which we so easily fall, we shall return to our primary goal of crossing the gain line in our journey towards a more balanced and harmonious life.

'Suffering is universal', as the Dalai Lama once wisely put it and, although we may strive for pleasure, perfection, and prosperity within our lives, it is only the happiness which comes from contentment that is truly sustainable. Even those born into privilege may find themselves subject to torment, heartbreak and anguish, and thus seeking material wealth as a path to happiness is often misguided, no matter how alluring such riches may appear to those of more modest origins. Irrespective of how expensive your car is, how luxurious your yacht may be, or how spectacular the view from your apartment, you are wherever you find yourself, and true happiness can only come from within. If actually given our heart's desires, we quickly become

desensitized to such pleasures and to what we see every day of our lives. Even champagne and caviar can become tiresome if consumed in excess.

If you are reading this book, the chances are that a certain *ennui*[36], or sense of frustration and futility may have entered your life. The goal of these chapters is to help you to understand the root causes of your present malaise and to introduce psychological and philosophical changes which will enable you to move your life in a more positive direction.

At any given point, we may come to find ourselves trapped within a set of daily rituals and routines which sap our time and energy and appear to prevent us from changing the course of our lives. However, as discussed within the preceding chapters, there are fundamental changes that we can make to the way in which we view our world and prioritize our affairs and, though these relatively simple changes, we can recover the time and energy needed to change course by **crossing the gain line**.

---

[36] 'feeling of listlessness and dissatisfaction arising from a lack of occupation or excitement'

Chapter Four

The daily reduction

"It's not the daily increase but the daily decrease. Hack away at the unessential." - Bruce Lee

The mantra of *'less is more'* may seem to have become more of a *cliché* than an apparent contradiction in terms. It is however of the greatest importance that this phrase becomes engrained within our guiding philosophy, and we will introduce a number of practical illustrations to lend clarity to this principle. As legend would have it, Bruce Lee, arguably one of the 20th Century's most unsung philosophers, was once asked how he approached his training. He famously remarked that he focused upon the daily reduction through the endless refinement of his training and methods. The secret to his success lay not in complexity, but rather in simplifying his technique and approach, thereby maximizing the efficiency and economy of his movements and daily routine. His philosophical approach to life helped him to gain fame, fortune, family and friends, and also to achieve an admirable balance between the professional and personal dimensions of his life.

We don't however need a guiding star like Bruce Lee to teach us the practicality of this principle. Every day, time and energy are wasted through inefficient conversations, long-winded Emails, unnecessary trips to the local store, and the needless repetition of tasks. For instance, how many hours would you have saved on trips to the convenience store last month if only you had made a list before departing[37]? Do we need to work out for an hour at the gym every day, or can we achieve the same results by training for half an hour three times a week? Is a lengthy Email really a more efficient form of communication, when a shorter, concise message is more likely to be read and assimilated and will take less time? How many times

---

[37] Try ColorNote from the App Store for a quick and easy way to create and update lists on the run

have you sent an original communication when a 'form letter' could simply have been modified? Can we learn a skill more quickly from short focused lessons? In this chapter we will expand upon the importance of this principle and apply it to many aspects of our daily lives.

Less work and more preparation

Whenever possible, do not undertake any activity or enterprise without first visualizing your objectives and contemplating the likely obstacles and outcomes. At first thought, this might appear a tiresome and pointless complication, but this approach will pay dividends. This form of meditative reflection is best done as one would daydream, relaxing one's conscious mind, and allowing the more powerful 'subconscious'[38] to envisage the many permutations that might arise. This 'dream state' is the best frame of mind in which to engage in such contemplation, and can be achieved while relaxing in a garden chair, resting quietly on a train, or soaking in a warm bath. Closing the eyes is often helpful, but it is the relaxation of the mind, and particularly the orbitofrontal cortex (which constantly integrates events and makes decisions)[39] that is of importance. A similar state of mind can be achieved simply by washing the dishes or 'zen gardening'[40]. As you wash the dishes with warm water or slowly rake the sand of the zen garden, allow your mind to relax and begin to visualize the task at hand, wandering through the various steps that you will likely have to navigate in order to achieve your intended goal. This is done in much the same way as you would visualize alternative routes to work or the various times of day when one road or another would be the quickest, or the most aesthetically pleasurable. This is a particularly useful exercise for developing this 'mind skill', one which is necessary to be able to visualize and solve complex problems without travelling to work or physically engaging with them. Even if you don't immediately come up with a clear answer, you will find that your subconscious mind has already been programmed and 'set to task' and, within a short period of time, the solution will usually spontaneously

---

[38] Malcolm Gladwell presents overwhelming evidence for the supremacy of the subconscious in 'Blink'
[39] 'Orbitofrontal cortex, decision-making and drug addiction', by Geoffrey Schoenbaum, Matthew Roesch & Thomas A. Stalnaker, Trends in Neuroscience Feb; 29(2): 116–124 (2006).
[40] A zen garden is a Japanese rock garden or dry landscape which is carefully arranged with sand that is raked to represent ripples in a body of water.

present itself. Spending thirty minutes visualizing your intended project with your eyes closed is far more efficient in terms of time and energy than spending hours trying to solve a problem without prior preparation. When you finally engage with the task you will find that you are more focused and effective in solving it.

'Victorious warriors win first and then go to war, while defeated warriors go to war first and then seek to win,' Sun Tzu[41]

The *'Art of War'* is regarded as a timeless classic by many scholars and strategists, but what makes it truly remarkable is the proportion of the book which is dedicated to planning, gathering intelligence, and delaying engagement until the most opportune moment. In fact, there are no descriptions of fighting methods or of battle tactics. Like Bruce Lee, Sun Tzu spends most of his time sharpening his philosophy rather than his sword. The ancient general impresses upon his reader the importance of minimizing the duration of war, and of striking only when ready and when all the prevailing factors are in your favour. While this might at first appear to advocate a rather militaristic approach to the world, his teachings are in fact applicable to our everyday lives, how we do business, and how we invest our time and energy. Sun Tzu watched and waited and understood all the prevailing elements of a situation prior to engagement or, to put it in his words, *'The general who wins the battle makes many calculations in his temple before the battle is fought. The general who loses makes but few calculations beforehand.'*

In a sense, life may be depicted as a daily struggle to cross the gain line and achieve an end result or, in other words, we strive to end every day further ahead than we were when we started it. However, as each passing day requires that we wash, dress, travel, eat, drink and perform countless little chores just to maintain our *status quo*, our daily struggle can be viewed as a battle against time. To employ a simple metaphor, imagine that your time and energy are

---

[41] 'The Art of War' by Sun Tzu

represented by running water and that the day is a colander. To ensure that some of your time and effort are retained, you to have to pour water into the colander at rate that is faster (or at least no slower) than the rate at which it drains out through the holes. While this analogy may appear to be 'negative', it nonetheless serves to convey the principle that, if we do not pour our efforts constantly into the day, then we will not obtain an end result which is above and beyond the starting point.

Thus, psychological preparation, focus and intensity are all essential if we are to escape the orbit of our daily routine and succeed in crossing the gain line. On a more positive note, this goal is made far easier if we waste less time during the course of our day, so that we may concentrate a greater proportion of our precious resources (i.e. our time, money and energy) in those directions which yield positive outcomes.

'If you do indeed love life, then do not waste time,' Bruce Lee

Refining our method as a route to greater efficiency

The mantra of quality over quantity should ring true for all aspects of our life, from our time at work to that we spend at the gym. Genuine gains only result through the refinement of our methods and techniques, rather than from the compulsion of *'putting in the hours'*. While *'practice may very well make perfect'*, there is simply no point in practising our mistakes or engaging in activities which can be either avoided or outsourced to those who are better at them. After all, insanity may alternatively be defined as *'repeating the same mistake over and over again and expecting a different outcome.'* Why not make a list of all those additional things that you try to do on a weekly or monthly basis, and eliminate those that are either unnecessary or could otherwise be outsourced to professionals?

For instance, let us take the case of Maggie, a recently divorced single mother who became weary of being 'a stay at home mother' and of her ex-husband's constant absenteeism. Maggie dreams of returning to her career path as a professional painter, but simply can't seem to find the time to sit down and paint, given her day job as a PA with two small children. She earns good money and receives generous alimony, but yearns to do something that she finds rewarding beyond the daily nine-to-six; she wants to return to spend more time in her studio so that she can re-join her beloved community of artists. However, at present, she is only able to find the odd afternoon or evening, and is trying to work out how much time she can salvage from her daily routine.

Maggie performs a simple exercise to see how much time she can recover for painting. She jots down the various elements of her daily routine to ascertain which activities or chores she can streamline or outsource without reducing her quality time with her children.

Old weekly schedule	New weekly schedule
Drive the kids to school	Organise community school run (2 hours/week)
Do crossword	Listen to audio book in car (1 hour/week)
Visit supermarket on way back	Order groceries online (2 hours/week)
Supervise kids' homework	Hire home tutor on Craig's List (4 hours/week)
Lunchbreak with colleagues	Spend lunch organising weekend activity for kids (6 hours/week)
Hour daily at gym	Three half hour sessions at gym (4 hours/week)
Cooking evening meal for family	Hire evening help for kids & cooking (10 hours/week)
	Paint in studio 2 hours/evening and 10 hours/weekend

Rather than driving the children to and from school as part of her commute, she decides to organise a 'car pool' rota with some other families in the neighbourhood to reduce her daily diversion to two days a week, thereby saving around two hours a week. Rather than adhering to her habit of rising at six and doing the crossword every morning, she instead elects to listen to audio books narrated by her favourite artists or to watch videos on her iPad to gain inspiration and learn new painting methods. Rather than visiting the supermarket every day on the way back from the school run, she decides to order all groceries online from now on, saving an additional two hours a week. For the past three years she has spent at least an hour every evening helping her children with their homework, but now she begins to realise that she is not a particularly gifted maths tutor or very adept at science and Spanish, and so Maggie decides to hire a home tutor from Craig's List. Instead of spending every lunch break chatting with her friends at the office, she elects to use one lunchtime each week to organize supervised weekend trips for her kids on a Saturday or a Sunday afternoon, thereby liberating a further six hours a weekend.

As for the rituals of food preparation, Maggie takes the decision to hire a cook for two hours every evening so that she can spend more quality time with her children. In relation to exercise, rather than driving to the gym at nine o'clock every night for an hour after putting the children to bed *(a practice which leaves her drained in the mornings)*, she decides to train for three half hour sessions a week during her lunch hour, as the gym is located only a five-minute walk from the office. This change in routine should recoup an additional four hours per week. She reasons that much of the additional cost of a tutor and a cook can be recovered by selling some of her artworks online. As she has now rescued an estimated nineteen hours from her weekly routine, Maggie can now devote two hours an evening to unwinding in her studio and a further ten hours at the weekend.

How much lost time can you reclaim from your weekly routine?

Why intensity outperforms volume

When it comes to exercise, it may not come as a complete surprise that *less proves to be more*. In controlled trials of cardiovascular *(aerobic)* exercise, intended to determine whether it is an increase in the intensity, frequency, or the duration of exercise which yields the best returns in terms of fitness, it has been shown that we respond most gainfully to more intense training than we do to more frequent or longer sessions[42]. Thus there is strong evidence that, in trials of intensity versus frequency and duration, *intensity prevails. Somehow this finding appeals to our intuitive reason, or 'common sense',* without the need to pore through the vast biomedical literature for a detailed physiological explanation.

Intense exercise, or rather placing a stress or 'load' upon our cardiovascular and musculoskeletal system, triggers the release of hormones which inform the tissues of the body of the need to increase capacity in order to meet future demands. However, exercise itself, other than being the stimulus for growth, only serves to drain our energy reserves and causes at least some damage to our joints, muscles and connective tissues *(which we sense as aches and pains).* Thus the replenishment of lost reserves and the repair of tissues *must precede any growth* during the recovery phase after exercise. While intense exercise may be the stimulus for growth, contrary to widely held misconceptions, we do not actually grow bigger, stronger, or faster during exercise, but rather as a consequence of recovery from exercise which necessitates sufficient rest and adequate nutrition. So, if we train less frequently and more intensively, we see better results *and save time and energy.* Conversely, if we make the same mistake as many inexperienced athletes, we will could experience an actual decline in performance and strength due to overtraining which, in extreme cases, can even result in rhabdomyolysis[43].

> *"You must understand that the workout does not actually produce muscular growth. The workout is merely a trigger that sets the body's growth mechanism into motion. It is the body itself, of course, that produces growth; but it does so only during a sufficient rest period."* Mike Mentzer[44]

Within the arcane world of bodybuilding *(which we visit only for the purposes of illustration)* there was once a great controversy surrounding the question of whether less was indeed more. According to bodybuilding folklore, this clash of titans was considerable and still resonates to

---

[42] Wenger HA, Bell GJ. The interactions of intensity, frequency and duration of exercise training in altering cardiorespiratory fitness. Sports Med. 1986 Sep-Oct;3(5):346-56.
[43] The breakdown of skeletal muscle tissue from extreme physical exercise.
[44] Champion bodybuilder and architect of high intensity training (1951-2001)

this day, keeping its disciples deep in conversation over their protein shakes to this day. Essentially, this debate distilled down to whether extreme physiques required extreme workouts in terms of volume and intensity. Joe Weider, ringmaster of his famed international bodybuilding circus, argued that champion physiques only came from Herculean workouts, not only in terms of the size of the weights that were lifted, but also how many 'sets of repetitions' were performed and how frequently. Weider's elected champions, including Arnold Schwarzenegger himself, advocated performing two workouts of two hours every day, six days a week, and consuming vast quantities of protein rich supplements[45]. In direct contradiction, Mike Mentzer devised the High Intensity Workout[46] in which he performed only 7 to 9 intense sets per session, three days a week, instead recommending a more moderate, balanced, and carbohydrate rich diet. Whether Joe Weider's vast 'pyramid workouts' and special dietary supplements *(which he sold and marketed)*, or Mike Mentzer's extremely brief, intense workouts are indeed the route to a massive muscular physique remains a heated debate. However, given that both Mike Mentzer and Arnold Schwarzenegger won the coveted Mr Olympia title (owned by Joe Weider), it could be argued that Mr Mentzer's intense minimalism did indeed prove that you can achieve equivalent results with less overall effort. We shall however leave the last word with Mr Mentzer.

"Many athletes sell themselves short, erroneously attributing their lack of satisfactory progress to a poverty of the requisite genetic traits, instead of to their irrational training and dietary practices and they give up training. Don't make the same mistake."

Why six small meals a day are better than one large one

Less has also proven to be more in relation to diet, especially in maintaining a healthy, balanced lifestyle. Eating large meals results in a greater proportion of the blood being diverted to the

---

[45] Joe Weider's Bodybuilding System (2001)
[46] High-Intensity Training the Mike Mentzer Way (2002)

liver and intestines, and we naturally tend to feel bloated and less inclined towards physical or mental activity, as the circulation carries fats and other more soluble breakdown products to the various organs of the body. Consuming a meal which is rich in carbohydrates triggers the release of insulin into the circulation, which stimulates glucose uptake into the fat, liver and muscle tissues, and reduces fat metabolism by the muscles. So, if we consume a meal that is rich in both fats and carbohydrates, we unsurprisingly tend to gain weight. However, if we eat many smaller meals a day, or continuously graze on healthy snacks when hungry (rather than sitting down for two or three major meals a day), our metabolism tends to gather pace and we avoid a loss of energy and lethargy. In fact, reducing our daily calorific intake by as much as 30% of the 'recommended daily intake', or RDI, otherwise known as *calorie restriction*, has been demonstrated to significantly extend the lifespan of every species studied, from worms to humans.[47] Truly, in terms of longevity, less has proven to be more…

The Pentagon's hard lesson

The modern American military has become somewhat fixated by the power of intelligence, and especially by the use of sophisticated surveillance networks of satellites, spy planes and drones to provide a complete 360° view of the battlefield. This 'total' coverage of the theatre of war and constant flow of information on the movements of planes, ships and tanks in 'real time' was supposed to make the world's largest military invincible, or so it was believed. Armed with this massive torrent of data, the U.S. military called in retired Marine General Paul Van Riper to play the role of the enemy, or 'red forces', in its Gulf War simulation known as 'Millennium Challenge 2002'.

It was General Van Riper's hardened military experience in Vietnam which had taught him that it was the devolution of authority, rather than the centralisation of command, that worked best on the battlefield. From fighting the Vietcong, he had also learned that the largest, most technologically sophisticated, and most 'powerful' military force does not always prevail in war.

---

[47] 'Calorie restriction, SIRT1 and metabolism: understanding longevity' by Laura Bordone & Leonard Guarente, Nature Reviews Molecular Cell Biology 6, 298-305 April (2005)

Trusting his individual commanders on the ground to perform their pre-arranged orders, General Van Riper adopted an 'old school' strategy to teach the younger generation of generals a hard lesson.

Rather than employing digital communication networks, General Van Riper used motorcycle messengers to convey his orders, and light signals to launch warplanes without the need for tell-tale radio communications that could be picked up the enemy. Having received an ultimatum to surrender within 24 hours, he was made aware of an impending attack, and directed a fleet of small fishing boats to determine the whereabouts of the allied fleet and sink it with a massive bombardment of cruise missiles, destroying the remnant of the ships with a flotilla of small red boats which could not be readily detected by the radar of 'blue' forces. Rumour has it that he also destroyed the allied landing grounds. Having dealt such a massive and crippling defeat upon the allied forces, he was then ordered to follow a pre-arranged script so that the blue forces could prevail as originally envisaged. Despite only being an expensive 'exercise', this undoubtedly came as a massive shock to the Pentagon. Military machismo aside, this exercise substantiated Marine General Paul Van Riper's *implicit* belief that too much information is not a good thing, and sometimes having rather less information of a higher quality is in fact more 'informative' than a great hum of battlefield 'noise'. Once again, less has been demonstrated to be more...

Use fewer words more carefully

The old adage that we should 'choose our words carefully' is perhaps truer today than it ever was. Not only is this wisdom a path to a more peaceful life, but choosing fewer words, more carefully, is also a far more effective and efficient method of communication. In this day and age, we are literally bombarded with messages from the moment we awake to the time we retire to bed. Whether it is the case, as darkly hinted by some science fiction writers, that certain disorders of the nervous system are caused by the modern avalanche of electronic information[48], there can be little doubt that we are exposed to far more daily communications than our forefathers. Although the digital revolution has greatly increased the speed of information, it also means that we spend proportionately far more of our working day (as well as our free tIme) engaged in electronic messaging rather than in producing 'useful' work.

In what now seems a distant age, the effort required to write or manually type personal letters meant that we sent fewer messages and, when we did, we placed much greater emphasis upon the tone and content of our communications. More time was spent writing, preparing and posting letters, and these took a great deal longer to arrive (rather like modern international bank transfers) and, as a consequence, we took much more time to read and reflect upon what we were going to say than actually saying it. As a result, communications were generally of a higher quality and we were less likely to be prone to rash remarks or ill-advised 'selfies'. Now that individuals are actually being fired or sued over images and posts made on Facebook and Twitter, not to mention inappropriate Emails to colleagues or students, it might be worth reflecting on why we feel so pressured to send so many communications or to respond quite so swiftly.

Electronic mail, or Email, was not originally intended to serve as a chat room or to become a digital 'conversation'. It was simply designed to be a far more rapid and efficient digital alternative to postal communications, memos and telegrams. For all other purposes, it was envisaged to serve much the same purpose, with an identifiable individual sending a communication to a recipient at a specified address. Well, judging by the number of unsuccessful deliveries and wrong addresses, and by the fact that mail is still routinely intercepted, tampered with, or read by unintended parties, little has really changed, except for the fact that when we had to hand type or write a letter and pay for postage, we were less inclined to dash off a message and then realise that we had forgotten to mention something and then hurry home to write another one and rush back to the post office for more stamps. Accordingly, the etiquette of letters was perhaps more civilized, as you were not expected to respond too quickly or too often. As a consequence, trains of communications often took

---

[48] William Gibson, 'Johnny Mnemonic', 1986

weeks or even months to conclude. Amusing as this might seem today, this meant that important matters were rarely resolved without due deliberation, and letters riddled with offensive remarks or legally inadvisable statements, written in the 'heat of the moment', were far fewer, largely because people remembered that they were legal communications which could be presented as evidence within a court of law.

So how do we break the newly engrained habit of sending Emails 'off the cuff', and overcome the feeling of guilt that accompanies leaving an Email unanswered for hours. Apart from the efficiency gains that come from 'batching' Email responses (which will be touched upon in greater detail in Chapter Seven), we frequently find that electronic correspondence is often fragmented over many instalments throughout the course of the day, and that it is much more sensible to collate many Emails from one sender into a single response, as this tends to improve the effectiveness of our communications. If it is a truly urgent matter, then 'people' will generally tend to call. Remember that the pause between a message and our response to it is the critical window which empowers us to control our agenda and plan our time more effectively, principally by not changing our schedule in response to sudden demands. If you cannot break the inherent feeling of guilt that you are somehow ignoring someone by not responding instantly to an Email, then set up an autoresponder that acknowledges their communication and details the time by which you will likely reply to them. One might even advocate responding to Emails no more than twice a day, and ideally only once, as, by this time, many of them will have become irrelevant, or been contradicted, clarified, or retracted.

As social media expands the reach of our networks, so we have less quality time to give to any one individual acquaintance. It could be argued that, if we have less time for each of our friends and associates, then we should at least ensure that the time we do spend is of the highest possible quality.

Can we learn more from short focused bursts than the long hour?

Classical education in the West has long been constructed based upon the assumption that longer classes are a more efficient way of communicating ideas; whether this be a forty-minute lesson in the schoolroom or a full hour spent in the lecture theatre. Without exploring the complexities of the human attention span, or our ability to learn solely by passively listening to a speaker, we will simply challenge the Western educational model by arguing that the human mind is wired to explore and experiment rather than to assimilate and absorb. It could be suggested that the modern Western education system is based upon a social and political agenda rather than an optimised way of learning. At present, courses and their various classes follow an agenda of what must be learned based upon a previously agreed syllabus (which has often been set years in advance). However, rather than basing the education system on an outdated agenda of what must be learned on which set of topics within a given number of lessons, it might be more productive to restructure the learning process by asking a series of key questions. After all, education is based upon the enquiring nature of the human mind. For instance, rather than giving a series of four one hour lectures on the cardiovascular system and a weighty reading list of books and papers, you could ask a group of medical students how the heart responds to the increased demands of exercise, or is able to simultaneously drive the circulation of both fresh and exhausted blood around the body? This would set their minds into motion and lead them to conduct their own independent research by scanning through the gigabytes of images and information which is available online. Instead of engaging in four hours of monologue, the teacher could then chair a group discussion for half an hour to ask the students questions and respond to their 'informed' answers, increasing both their level engagement and their understanding of the topic.

In a similar vein, one can learn more about a topic by researching it with a specific question or 'framework' in mind, than by pulling a book off a shelf and starting to read from chapter one. If your question is why does the *'sous vide' (vacuum)* cooking technique improve the perceived flavour of food or, what enzymes tenderize meat and which specific fruits or spices contain them, then you are more likely to gain an understanding of the nature of protein structure in meat than you would by reading a hundred learned journal articles on the biochemical properties of skeletal muscle *(and of course obtain the desired answer far more quickly)*. When reading around or researching a topic on the Internet, it is always more purposeful to have a question in mind before beginning, or it is otherwise very easy to lose one's way when navigating the vast seas of knowledge.

Perhaps more importantly, knowledge has become largely obsolete within our new digital age of information. This tends to render classical learning techniques rather obsolete. After all, if you need to know something specific, you can now summon the information in an instant simply by uttering the magic phrase 'OK Google'. However, what separates the focused and effective seeker of knowledge from the wandering mind is the *understanding* of the information retrieved; the ability to place it into *context;* and the capacity to *filter out the 'noise'* of unwanted information from the answer that is being sought.

It is truly impressive what the prepared and focused human mind can achieve within a very short span of time. You can scan a hundred faces within a minute to identify a suspect; type the storyline for an entire book within ten; or sort all of your online contacts within a social network into discrete social circles within a quarter of an hour, based upon how you met them, and the nature of their connection to you. Imagine what your mind, when fully motivated and focused, could achieve within an intensely focused hour. For instance, you could learn to use a new software package to create images; compose and learn a new song; or write and memorize a short speech designed to leave a critical impression with a client or manager. When it comes to time, a focused mind achieves far more in less time...

Hopefully, having discussed this range of illustrations, you may finally be convinced that less is more within so many aspects of our lives. Why spend extra time and energy to achieve less?

Chapter Five

The importance of attaining a healthy work-life balance

While most of us tend to fall into extremes of excess or avoidance, some people seem to be very good at maintaining a healthy balance. This should not be perceived as an optional consideration, as occupying either end of the spectrum can be personally, professionally, and socially calamitous. For instance, whether they succeed or fail in their careers, *'workaholics'* tend to enter a tunnel of social isolation and, ultimately, come to the dread realization that life was 'all about the journey'. In contrast, those who are work shy, skipped much of school and took every weekend off, as well as every vacation and sick day that was available to them, often fall far behind the curve and miss out on many of life's precious opportunities.

Evidently life is about attaining a balance – an inescapable wisdom that was not lost upon the *'ancient'* philosophers who were privileged to be born into a world with so much time in which to think. Again, philosophy should not be viewed as an esoteric and obsolete branch of academia, one condemned to obscurity by the relentless advance of technology, but rather as the lens through which we view the world - a world which is, after all, merely a construct of our mind and senses. If our lens is cracked or opaque, then our view of the world will also be distorted, and our reactions to the events within it will often be inappropriate and result in misfortune rather than opportunity. Accordingly, it is perhaps worth briefly reviewing the ideas of some influential schools of philosophy to help us in constructing our own personal philosophy - one which is of some guidance in a complex world.

The long line of *stoics*, from Marcus Aurelius[49] to Zeno[50], essentially argued that we are merely vessels on the seas of fortune and should be indifferent to both pleasure and pain and, in general, accepting of life's various blessings and misfortunes. While such a philosophy may

---

[49] Meditations of Marcus Aurelius, Emperor of Rome, 161 - 180 AD
[50] Zeno of Cyprus, 334 - 262 BC

help us to come to terms with mishaps, failures and loss, or even to find contentment, it is nonetheless a rather negative philosophical outlook, one which denies our capacity for creativity, our ability to heal, our active desire to seize opportunities, and our capacity to influence our own destinies.

The rise of the school of stoicism was preceded by the philosophies of Confucius[51], whose teachings emphasized the importance of morality within all aspects of our personal and professional lives. The ancient Chinese sage advocated a code of conduct within all our relationships, as well as the primacy of justice and sincerity in creating a harmonious society. His concept of the *'moral imperative'* was later adopted by Immanuel Kant, whose *'golden rule'* that *'one should treat others as one would like to be treated'*, is merely a paraphrased version of Confucius' wisdom. However, it does enable him to explain why the teachings of Christ and the Buddha are of fundamental importance if we are to achieve a balanced and fair society. Put simply, if most of us behave in a dishonest or immoral way, for instance by 'gaming the system', cheating on our partners, or evading our taxes then, even if we are not discovered, our society would eventually collapse into chaos and disorder, as such conventions are the supporting columns of a stable civilisation. You only have to cast your mind back to the recent events of the Global Financial Crisis, or to the widespread arson and looting that were characteristic of the riots of London and Los Angeles to understand the point that is being made.

Within a stable and 'law abiding' society, we agree to conform to a number of social conventions over and above the established laws of the state, which collectively amount to a 'code of conduct'. Such codes of conduct evolve within cultures over time in the interests of the 'common good' and to maintain mutual respect and decency. These 'rules' therefore serve to establish the lines or limits of the 'game of life' in which we all seek, either individually or cooperatively, to maximize our opportunity and advantage. As an academic exercise, viewing the world in terms of 'game theory' has proven to be revealing for psychologists and economists[52], but it nonetheless denies the existence of that which is intrinsically human -

[51] The Analects of Confucius, 551 – 479 BC
[52] 'Games, Rationality and Behaviour: Essays on Behavioural Game Theory and Experiments' by Alessandro Innocenti & Patrizia Sbriglia (2008)

namely our moral and 'spiritual' dimension, and that spark of disruptive creativity which we call 'genius'[53].

'We are unique, in that we create ourselves...

we forge ourselves in the fire of our will.'

We can certainly argue that contentment is very much a virtue, and that a law-abiding citizen is a good citizen. It is also reasonable to suggest that long-suffering souls are 'admirable' in terms of their resilience and the fortitude of their character. However, such philosophies of forbearance and silent suffering do not drive change within ourselves, our lives, or our society. It would seem unlikely that Martin Luther, Nicolas Tesla, or Henry Ford were devotees of such schools of thought. Great social reformers, inventors and entrepreneurs are notable for their driving ambition and their will to effect change within their lives and the lives of others. Many of those entrepreneurs who have transformed our world may not be widely perceived as powerful intellectuals, but their philosophies certainly were. Often the clarity of their vision was what made them so effective and perhaps this is why we refer to them as 'visionaries'. It is their simplifying philosophy and clarity of thought that enables them to ignore the 'background noise' of the world and focus upon attaining their goals through a process of transformation. This was a gift that was often attributed to those who practised the ancient art of purification known as alchemy[54].

For the purposes of constructing our own philosophy, we might reasonably suggest that any essentially *'fatalistic'* ideology is unlikely to aid us in improving our lives, or indeed in fulfilling the vision of the founding fathers of the United States of America, which was the pursuit of a full life, liberty and happiness. However, for us to effect change within our external lives, we must first change ourselves. It is only once this has been achieved that we expect to change

---

[53] From the Latin *genius,* meaning *spirit*
[54] The Alchemist, Paulo Coelho (1998); The book of Alchemy, Francis Melville (2002)

our circumstances, which will then empower us to change the world around us. As the late, great Stephen R. Covey once put it, *'personal victories always precede public victories'.*

'Men's natures are alike - it is their habits that carry them far apart.' - Confucius

The essential elements of a balanced life

Whether we refer to happiness, contentment, or what Confucius calls 'harmony', what we are essentially discussing is a life in 'balance'. A few among us appear to be able to balance the various dimensions of our lives fairly effortlessly, although most of us simply retreat to the security of our strengths. For instance, those who feel most comfortable with their working status and intellectual pursuits may spend most of their waking lives either reading books or computer screens - individuals we used to refer to as 'bookworms' – people who either passively or actively shun social contact. In a similar vein, those who crave love, affection and companionship may err on the side of excessive socialization at the expense of their work and other obligations. The lives of such people often fall into a state of disrepair and dependency.

For us to achieve harmony, we must first seek to attain balance within the six dimensions of our lives; namely the professional *(the need to make a living and remain productive)*; personal *(our 'spiritual' need to read, reflect and meditate)*; social *(as we are by definition a social species)*; romantic *(the requirement for intimacy and companionship)*; intellectual *(sharpening the mental tools necessary for our survival)*; and the physical *(as we have to maintain a healthy body to function effectively)*.

It is human nature to pursue 'success' and to overindulge our senses when opportunity presents itself. Yet our senses tire quickly, and too much pleasure may not only be a 'bad thing' - it is also a biological certainty, as the pleasure and reward systems of our midbrain (which are mediated by the release of dopamine[55]) soon desensitize, as any addict will recount from their

---

[55] The Functional Neuroanatomy of Pleasure and Happiness, Morten L. Kringelbach & Kent C. Berridge, 2010

attempts to relive their early euphoric experiences. In fact, this ancient centre of the brain helps to explain how and why certain personal and social behaviours are reinforced through the process of reward. From such studies it becomes profoundly clear just how easy it is to condition individuals towards 'socially approved' behaviours simply by reinforcing 'positive outcomes' in the form of promotions and awards, or by strengthening desirable conduct through the provision of social dinners, luxury commodities, and 'sex'. Unsurprisingly, we are prone to becoming 'approval addicts', constantly seeking affirmation and acknowledgement from those who administer our rewards and govern our futures, whether these taskmasters be our parents, our employers, or the heads of an organized crime syndicate. As a consequence, many of us spend much of our time continuously seeking approval, while those who tend the purse strings 'hold court'. Our socioeconomic system, which is largely based on success and reward, therefore constitutes a powerful social construct - one whose epicentre is hard-wired deep within our central nervous system.

Perhaps it is also understandable that we seek to reinforce our successes and avoid our failures. If a businessman is successful in making money and gaining social notoriety from doing so, even though he may be 'unlucky in love', it may prove tempting for him to pursue more of the same, thereby avoiding the pitfalls of intimate relationships, instead preferring the transient rewards of material prosperity in his quest for 'social affirmation'. This is another illustration of the power of social conditioning, as we are all by nature 'risk averse', instinctively drawn towards those rewards which are more readily obtained.

We can only really reap the benefits of a full harvest if we distribute our time and energies across all the various dimensions of our lives. If we exercise or perform physical labour without rest then we soon become exhausted; while if we eat, drink or party excessively then we feel ill and lose our mental and physical vitality; yet if we think or work too hard then we become withdrawn and are unable to enjoy the fruits of our labours. How can we ever be truly happy if our lives are constantly out of balance?

Achieving a life balance

In order to achieve this balance, we have to continuously assign time and effort to every aspect of our lives, every single week, by ensuring that we engage in at least one activity for each dimension. This is understandably hard to do, as it means stepping out of our 'comfort zone' and trying things that we are not necessarily good at or have been previously unsuccessful in doing.

'Genius is one percent inspiration and ninety-nine percent perspiration.' - Thomas A. Edison

A practical perspective

We are not all born equal, whether we consider equality in terms of wealth, education, opportunity, or genetic potential. Although prodigies like Mozart, Newton & Picasso may all have been exceptionally gifted, they still worked themselves to exhaustion in order to realize their full potential. Thus, even for those exceptional geniuses amongst us, the principle of the 'ten-thousand-hour rule' still applies, even if this might be marginally reduced in a few celebrated cases.

Rare phenomena aside, we all possess great potential to develop new skills and aptitudes, and stem cells[56] continue to be produced well into our eighties. Stem cells are the endlessly dividing precursors of new muscle, skin, blood and brain tissue, and thus our capacity to acquire new abilities essentially never disappears, even if our desire to do so fades. In other words, much of the decline we commonly associate with aging occurs through disuse rather than an actual loss of capacity. For those who have always wondered, the answer is yes, we can learn new tricks...

We shall approach each of the six dimensions in more practical terms within the following paragraphs.

---

[56] Stem Cells: A Cellular Fountain of Youth, Mark P. Mattson and Gary Van Zant, 2002

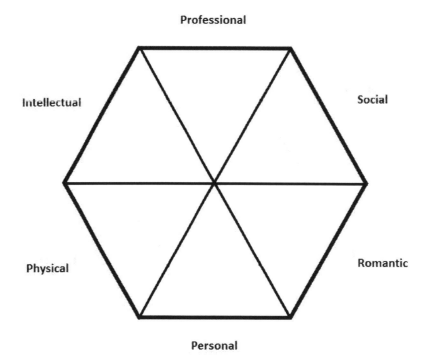

The physical dimension

When we raise the subject of *'physical exercise'*, we do not mean to suggest that we should seek to become exemplary athletes, or push ourselves to a pinnacle of fitness that can be tracked and monitored by the latest generation of smart watches. What this does mean is that we should commit ourselves to participate in some form of physical activity or exercise at least three times a week, especially if our way of life means that we are sedentary for most of the day. Everyone has a physical outlet which appeals to them, whether this be walking, tennis, swimming, jogging, golf or attending the gym for three sessions a week. We may even develop a 'healthy addiction' to such activity, which will in turn enable us to feel more energetic in our pursuit of life's other dimensions. A lack of physical fitness can profoundly affect our drive and self-confidence within the various aspects of our daily life, and thus we should come to regard attaining a level of fitness as a foundation stone in our efforts to restructure our lives and achieve balance.

The intellectual dimension

Just as the body requires regular exercise to maintain its flexibility and capacity for work, so the brain also needs regular stimulation, given its role as our primary tool for survival and prosperity. In the same way as the body requires many forms of training to optimally condition its various muscles, including the heart, postural and skeletal muscles, so the brain requires visual, computational and creative stimulation - even if this means attending an opera performed in a foreign language and trying to follow the storyline. Anagrams, crosswords, Sudoku and other logic puzzles all serve as good staple fare, yet solving problems is an even more rewarding activity if this entails an end product, such as writing a book, constructing a model, filming a documentary, learning a new language, or creating a work of art. Instead of watching the standard Hollywood evening fare, why not watch a documentary, or an arts film which challenges the senses with a friend, and then discuss it over dinner or a drink? If you are struggling for an idea or to make a start, why not search for an evening class or activity group on Meetup.com, Gumtree.com or Craig's List? If you like books then join a book club or, if chess is your passion, then why not make it a more social one? Spend at least an hour a day or two three two hour sessions a week, developing what might alternatively be referred to as a 'hobby'. However, one should never forget the true purpose of the exercise, which is to hone and sharpen your creative intellect.

The social dimension

The human brain is a complex and highly flexible organ, one which has taken hundreds of millions of years to develop and refine. It has the capacity to store memories, construct visual images, coordinate complex movements, and even localize the origin of sounds. What elevates us above all other species is not our opposable thumbs or the development of language (which other species also possess), but rather the extent to which our frontal cortex has expanded - a development which has enabled us to create the most advanced and complex society on the planet. With so much of our brain dedicated to higher social function[57] – including the ability to read subtle facial expressions, reflect empathy, construct complex social interactions, and even listen in on a specific conversation at a party (the so-called *'cocktail party effect'*[58]) – it would certalnly appear an oversight not to make constructive use of such a large proportion of the functional capacity of our brains.

Any disruption to our normal socialization which is caused by a dysfunction of the brain may have serious consequences. For this reason, it is perhaps unsurprising that such social dysfunctions comprise most of the entries that may be found within the psychiatrists' 'bible'[59]; mental maladies that range from significant impairments, including depression and mild autism, to debilitating conditions such as psychosis and schizophrenia. Accordingly, we have to employ and develop all aspects of our brain function in order to maintain them in a healthy functional state and avoid losing our 'sharpness of mind'. At a more practical level, this means putting ourselves into the forefront of group conversations and activities rather than sitting on the side-lines. *'Politics'* or, as an alternative definition, the 'social economics of human interaction and competition for resources' *(which may include, but are not limited to, money, space, food and access to sexual partners)*, is an inescapable aspect of our social reality and, if we take a step back or withdraw, then we risk losing out altogether. Thus we have to actively engage on a social level in order to present ourselves within a good light and not to become misrepresented as being reclusive, arrogant, or evasive. Always remember that the human imagination abhors a vacuum. Those who disengage from the world – known as the *'hikikomori'*[60] in Japan – stand to miss out on many social and professional opportunities and usually fail to thrive. Some of these individuals may even go on to develop such antisocial behaviours as hacking and voyeurism, or addictions to 'virtual unrealities' like pornography or video games.

---

[57] 'Meeting of minds: the medial frontal cortex and social cognition', David M. Amodio & Chris D. Frith, Nature Reviews Neuroscience 7, 268-277 (April 2006)
[58] The Cocktail Party Effect in Auditory Interfaces, Lisa J. Stifelman, 1994.
[59] The Diagnostic and Statistical Manual of Mental Disorders (DSM), American Psychiatric Association.
[60] The phenomenon of reclusive adolescents or adults.

Many of us, often as a result of a setback or disappointment, become a little reticent or 'shy' in social situations, especially around those we don't know particularly well. Irrespective of such 'knocks', it is of the greatest importance that we seek to regain our social footing and make an effort towards a greater and wider level of social engagement and, most crucially, that this should not solely occur through the virtual interface of social media. Although Facebook, LinkedIn and Tinder might be wonderful tools for finding people who are of prospective interest to us, they do not convey the *sincerity* of direct personal interaction, or convey the opportunities that may come from personal encounters. While your presence on social media may well win you an interview or a date, few people of interest are likely to make a direct investment in you based solely upon such a virtual interaction. As humans *we need* personal interactions. Being able to read one another's facial expressions, hear one another's voices, and sense those key gestures and intonations is essential if we are to form meaningful social bonds or feel able to invest in a relationship.

When it comes to developing social skills or social presence, there is simply no alternative to total immersion in social situations. To dive in at the deep end, why not find a 'Meetup' group online and engage with people of similar interest at least once a week, or invite those within your local community around for a meal or barbeque? You will soon get to know (and like) most of your neighbours, and any wariness or distrust is soon dispelled by open communication. Remember that most conflicts are triggered by a failure of communication and most commonly arise from disrespecting social boundaries and conventions. We must be mindful that even the slightest disrespect of another person - for example 'jumping the queue' - can result in an altercation, as you are in effect disrespecting someone else and, by subconscious inference, are placing yourself on a higher plane of the 'totem pole'. All groups of individuals tend to arrange themselves into a hierarchy of standing instinctively - which we may refer to as a social dominance hierarchy[61] - albeit with a great deal of subtlety in terms of posturing and behaviour. We are readily able to divine the physical form and stature of another individual, but it is an acquired skill to do so using the peripheral vision so as not to

---

[61] Social Dominance: An Intergroup Theory of Social Hierarchy and Oppression, Jim Sidanius & Felicia Pratto (Cambridge University Press)

appear to 'notice' or 'stare impolitely'. Developing this skill is useful if we are to avoid giving the impression of making a social 'judgement', however subtle or unintentional it may be. We may not be aware, for instance, that we have made a negative facial expression or engaged in a rude or inappropriate stare, as our eyes often betray our curiosity and innermost desires. For those who wish to actively hone their social skills and develop a greater social presence and awareness, there are few activities that match the effectiveness of acting classes or joining a debating society. Social skills matter immensely - even if we do elect to choose our theatres of social engagement carefully.

The romantic dimension

The word romantic has been chosen carefully, in a deliberate effort to avoid making direct reference to the complex realm of human sexuality. We should remember that, although sex may well be a positive and healthy aspect of a full adult life, it should not be considered an essential part of our daily or weekly routine. It should certainly never be regarded as a right or expectation. We will inevitably endure 'barren spells' owing to natural cycles in our health and the making and breaking of relationships, especially given that we too have reproductive seasons and monthly cycles of fertility. What we *do need* as sentient human beings, is the intimacy of physical touch and the therapeutic release of close personal relationships. As social beings we have a fundamental need to belong and to feel that we are accepted. Social confidence and intimacy are merely deeper aspects of this interpersonal bonding. In short, intimate, tactile, physical relationships are simply essential to our well-being[62]. To illustrate the point more emphatically, infants that are not touched or handled eventually die[63]. It should come as no surprise that so many of us become socially dysfunctional or emotionally affected when we are excluded from the rituals of social bonding and the comforting reassurance of human touch.

---

[62] The Science of Intimate Relationships, G.J.O. Fletcher, J.A. Simpson, L. Campbell, & N., (2012) Wiley.
[63] http://www.nytimes.com/1988/02/02/science/the-experience-of-touch-research-points-to-a-critical-role.html?pagewanted=all

Some of us will already have been fortunate enough to have found our soul mates and be especially strong within this dimension. However, others among us are not so skilled at the social rituals of dating and mating. There are those of us who have been emotionally scarred by a formative relationship, others who have been rejected by their peer groups, and some who will have endured a particularly loveless or abusive childhood. Whatever the disappointment, we need to actively seek to reengage with society to build empathic relationships and restore ourselves within a circle of trust. One of the ways in which our capacity to trust can be restored is by joining a sensual massage group, an activity which cultivates intimacy and breaks down our inhibitions in relation to human contact. For those who are not yet ready for such a bold leap, there are non-contact alternatives such as speed dating and 'lock & key' parties, although even this presents a daunting challenge for some of us who have lost confidence. The good news is that are myriad dating sites which pander to every social and sexual niche of society, and these are but a few well-chosen search terms and a click of the mouse away...

The personal dimension

To achieve balance, we need to pause and reflect upon events and our reactions to them. Without balance in our lives, we will eventually trip upon our misjudgements and invariably fall. In more worldly terms, this means that we will say the wrong thing to the wrong person or make a costly miscalculation. We will not dwell here on the undoubted benefits of *meditation* and the wisdom of its practitioners, or recap on the importance of *sleep*. *Reflection* is however essential if we are to *make sense* of the events which have taken place and be able to *rationalise* where we may have gone wrong and what we could have done better. Allowing our minds to relax and drift over the day's developments during moments of calm is an essential habit if we are to be able to plan our next steps forward with clarity. We need quieter moments, in the absence of haste, to visualize our goals and keep account of our progress.

Some of the most valuable moments you will ever pass are those spent within this 'zone' of reflective thought. In this mode a 'bridge' is opened between the conscious and 'subconscious' minds, and we are able to employ the full power of our brain to visualise, evaluate and project events from the past through the present and far into the future. In this state we can view the world and our experiences within it through what the ancients referred to as the 'mind's eye.' Once this bridge has been opened, we can achieve a clarity of thought which enables us to penetrate the fog and chaos of the world. This state of mind is most readily achieved when relaxing on a couch or in a garden chair, or when immersed in a warm bath or lying under the summer sun. Within this state your mind is free to wander through memories of past or recent events, and to adjudge them as having been gainful or undesirable, avoidable or unavoidable, and well-handled or poorly-judged. By means of this memory 'replay' you can reconstruct specific highlights and then proceed to deconstruct how things could have gone better, and which key moments were pivotal to how events unfolded. The practice of **ideation** is invaluable, and is also key to the planning process. *Ideation* is the forming of ideas or images within the mind, and your subconscious is far better than your active working brain (the pre-frontal cortex which deals with immediate decisions, interactions and calculations) at this. For those who desire to learn more about the power of the subconscious mind, the topic is discussed in fascinating detail by Malcolm Gladwell within his seminal work 'Blink'[64].

Within this state of mind, you should now be able to **ideate** your end goal and **visualise** how you are going to reach this destination through a series of specific actions and milestones. Visualize precisely what the target is, including where you will be and what you will be able to do once you have attained your objective. Between where you are now and your ultimate goal, you will be able to identify a number of obstacles that you will have to overcome in order to reach your destination, and also which skills or resources you will need to acquire or obtain to bring about this ambition. In this 'meditative state' our brains are highly efficient and we may make significant progress within only a few minutes of quiet contemplation. Before you embark upon any major undertaking, practice this art of ideation and visualization so that you learn to execute your goals effectively. What we are in effect doing is *programming* the mind to perform a set of tasks efficiently and effectively, only in this case *you are the programmer* and are determining your own destiny.

---

[64] Read 'Blink' by Malcolm Gladwell

The functioning of the human brain can be regarded as being analogous to that of a modern computer at many levels. Both have a short term memory, or cache, that requires emptying regularly or the system begins to malfunction. Sleep and meditation, rather like switching a computer to standby, are essential for ensuring healthy mental function and for the consolidation of useful information in the form of accessible memories. As with a computer, information can either be stored temporarily (within the frontal cortex of the brain or the cache of a computer) or else encoded within long-term memory. Existing memories can be erased or overwritten with new information or solutions (behaviours). As with a computer, the efficient functioning of the brain requires that all systems act together in concert. Like a computer, there exist deeply embedded programmes within the ancient structures of the brain which are essential to our basic functioning. On a computer these critical programmes are stored in and run from the read only memory (ROM), whereas such operating systems tend to be found within the more ancient parts of the human brain (such as the brain stem). In contrast, those programmes or behaviours which are more transient, or 'in the moment', tend to be stored and run from the more recent parts of the brain (the random access memory or RAM of a computer). Thus the brain, like a computer, has the ability to learn and forget skills that are only needed for a short period of time. Periodically our brains, like computers, need to be purged of old files and bad, unwanted memories, a process which is essential to our mental health.

Just like a computer, our brain can be overwhelmed and extended far beyond its normal capacity. For instance, we can try to store more information than we have the capacity to store, or we can attempt to do more tasks at the same time than we can process efficiently (*e.g.* 'multi-tasking'). Like computers, our minds can 'crash' or even suffer sudden catastrophic breakdowns. On the other side of the coin, our minds can be pre-programmed to function more efficiently, reprogrammed to perform more useful or gainful tasks *(than playing video games or watching nonsense)*, provided with good data *(rather than being filled with junk or viral content)*, and used altogether more constructively to achieve our end goals.

The professional dimension

Our **profession**, or what we do for money, might more usefully be viewed as our 'primary skill set'. As such, it should remain the most important aspect of our *daily* lives, at least until we can replace it with another, more satisfying, enterprise. The initial challenge is to prevent it from becoming an all-consuming activity, as it so often does. As a further note of caution, we should also be wary of seeking psychological security in what we do for a living, even though this provides us with a sense of social validation and reassurance. Within the many diverse walks of life, one of the first questions we are asked, especially by new acquaintances, is 'what do we do' for a living. The purpose of this enquiry is perhaps self-evident - it instantly 'defines' our socioeconomic status, and serves as a barometer of our means and social worth. It is therefore unsurprising that we find ourselves seeking refuge within our 'pay grade' and professional status, not only for the material comforts which they bestow upon us, but also for the social standing and confidence that derive from them.

As with any psychological 'bunker', it is easy to become deeply entrenched and seek security by locking oneself away within a professional stronghold *(even though our lives and fortunes are nothing if not transient in nature)*. We also tend to forget that we embarrass others, who may well endure a less secure financial footing, when we attempt to establish our professional status within a conversation. It is this firmly rooted need to seek validation that drives so many of us to work longer hours, often for little or no additional pay, simply to gain approval and our badges of professional acceptance. It is precisely this powerful form of social conditioning which prevents us from working more efficiently or from shifting our *modus operandi* towards a goal-orientated pattern of employment rather than one whose agenda is dominated by the need to appear to be putting in the 'prerequisite' number of hours.

In the complex game of life, we tend to deal in our strongest suit, as this is the one in which we usually compete most effectively for resources and opportunities. However, the key to addressing the issue that our professional lives are all-consuming is not to seek to work more intensively, or longer hours. The goal is to spend our office time more productively and to use the associated savings to ensure that we get out of the office on time. Efficiency is more than just a mind-set - it is a habit which is continuously cultivated and refined - and much of this book addresses strategies which help us to do so, including *batching* and *visualization*.

Crossing the gain line focuses upon philosophy and strategy (or *ways and means*) of achieving our primary goal, which is to spend more time enjoying what we do and less doing what we don't find particularly rewarding or engaging. The *focus* of this book is to *reduce the number of hours we work each day by increasing our efficiency and effectiveness* rather than developing strategies to maximise our incomes. As such we are not seeking to become materially rich but rather, as one South American gentleman once wisely put it, *'to become richer in other ways.'* The intention of this book is to recover more time for our friends and loved ones, and more time for what we enjoy doing the most. It should become our primary goal to become happier and healthier *by achieving a balance within our lives*, and it is very often our own internal programming – our social and psychological inhibitions - which prevent us from doing so.

There exist countless books which cover, in painstaking detail, how we can succeed in the commercial world[65], become rich[66], create our own 'lifestyle business'[67], or establish an online entity which generates income with the minimum of effort[68]. These are not however the objectives of this book. If become so fortunate as to amass personal wealth through our labours, whether by publishing books, creating spectacular artworks, or becoming a celebrity persona, then that is very much down to fate and the mood of the market. As Felix Dennis, the late master of poetry and publishing once put it, *'If the influence of luck is a delusion, then all I can say is that the delusion is virtually universal.'* Felix, during our brief acquaintance, would attest that he was one of the luckiest men alive, as almost every seed he had sown had culminated in a great harvest. However most of us will not be in the right place, at the right time, with the right idea, and the right product. Serendipity is a wonderful blessing, but it requires eons of wisdom and patience to cultivate, not to mention a great deal of luck. It is perhaps unwise to base your future investment strategies on the vicissitudes of fate, and most

---

[65] 'Enter the Dragon' by Theo Paphitis, 2008
[66] 'How to get Rich' by Felix Dennis, 2007
[67] 'Lifestyle Entrepreneur' by Jesse Krieger, 2014
[68] 'The Four Hour Work Week' by Timothy Ferris, 2011

people who succeed in the financial markets are of course very 'well-informed' by insiders. After all a wise investor only backs a horse if he or she knows it is going to win...

Money can be used for great good as well to fund less moral pursuits, although wealth usually tends to attract all the wrong kind of attention. Rather than pursuing a sun of gold, it is the mission of this book to enable us to spend our days doing something that we find rewarding, and to live somewhere we are at peace and with people we love. If we have our health and happiness and our lives are in a state of balance, then we can attain a state of bliss and there is little else we can reasonably ask for. Those who crave power, wealth or the endless pursuit of pleasure are destined to become psychological prisoners to such dark energies. We are, after all, merely human 'souls' on a journey from birth to our final resting place. We are all born, we all live, and we all die - the only difference being how and where, and why.

Perhaps it is best to conclude this chapter with another practical 'case study' to illustrate the simple steps which will enable us to achieve a more balanced life.

Charlie, a case in point

Charlie was very frustrated. As a qualified accountant in his mid-thirties, he spent the lion's share of his waking hours in the company office where he remains a valued member of the middle management team, shouldering considerable responsibility. However, Charlie's true passion lies in becoming a professional football[69] referee and, to this end, he spends as much time as possible at the weekends officiating local league matches. He runs up to ten miles a week to stay fit, and dreams of becoming a Premier League referee and one day of refereeing a cup final. Charlie has been divorced from his college sweetheart for some three years now, and secretly yearns for another soulmate. He doesn't want to give up his day job - but he would prefer to spend less time in the office so that he can complete his mission to become a professional referee. To achieve this goal, he needs to gain his higher refereeing qualifications (or badges), yet time is of the essence and he doesn't seem to have any to spare...

---

[69] Soccer rather than American or Australian Rules' football

Charlie's current timetable

	Monday	Tuesday	Wednesday	Thursday	Friday	Saturday	Sunday
8 am	Commute					Read newspapers	
9 am	Office						
10 am							
11 am						Travel to match	
noon						Pre-match preparations	
1 pm							
2 pm						Match officiating	
3 pm							
4 pm							
5 pm							
6 pm						Post-match events	
7 pm							
8 pm						'Mates' nights	
9 pm	Commute						
10 pm	Run	Run	Run	Run	Run		
11 pm	Evening meal						

As we can see from the previous incarnation of his weekly schedule *(presented above)*, Charlie was very much a stickler for routine. He would arrive at the office at 9 o'clock each morning after an hour's commute from the suburbs, and then work straight through until 8 or 9 in the evening without so much as a lunchbreak *(as his PA would bring sandwiches and snacks to his desk)*. He would then return home and go for an hour's run every night before bed. At the weekends he would rise late and then drive to a local league game, get changed, check the condition of the pitch and the match ball, and ensure that all was in order. Charlie usually officiated two games a weekend, and would then spend the evening drinking socially with his friends or the local league players. Charlie was very much a creature of habit and, although he largely spent his time doing what he loved, his life was simply not in balance and he was generally tired and unhappy.

Last September Charlie resolved to end the routine that had governed the previous six years of his life; one which had left him jaded and went some way towards explaining why his wife had left him. Charlie has since decided that endless meetings with his junior colleagues was not the best way to run his unit. Instead he has elected to delegate more responsibility and decision-making to his individual team leaders, thereby cutting the number of daily departmental meetings from three to just one or two. Charlie now aggregates his client calls into a single hour a day, and only answers his Emails in batches at 9 am, 1 pm (while eating a sandwich), and 5 pm, rather than 'on demand', as had been his habit. Such batching has freed his mind to focus upon client reports, now that he has effectively concentrated his electronic communications into two hours a day. Rather than being seen to be the last to leave the office in the evening, Charlie now departs the office at 6 pm promptly and heads straight for the nearby health club to exercise until 7 pm, thereby avoiding the height of the rush hour commute. These days he is usually home by 8 pm and spends two of his newly liberated hours studying for his higher referee's badge on Monday and Tuesday evenings, leaving the other three weekday evenings open for dates or evening football fixtures - whichever comes his way. Charlie has elected to join the popular dating site Match.com in his search for a soulmate, and now sets Saturday nights aside as potential 'date nights' rather than 'mates'[70] nights.

---

[70] 'mates' is the English vernacular for friends

Charlie's new look timetable

	Monday	Tuesday	Wednesday	Thursday	Friday	Saturday	Sunday
8 am	Morning commute					Read newspapers	
9 am	Office						
10 am							
11 am						Travel to match	
noon						Pre-match preparations	
1 pm							
2 pm						Match officiating	
3 pm							
4 pm							
5 pm							
6 pm	Evening gym session					Post-match events	
7 pm	Evening commute						
8 pm	Evening meal						
9 pm	FA advanced referee training course	Game or date night	Game or date night	Game or date night	Date night	'Mates' night	
10 pm							
11 pm	Online dating						

These days Charlie usually finds himself officiating at least one midweek game and two at the weekend, which he enjoys tremendously, and feels much less fatigued now that he is getting home at a more civilized hour and able to unwind with his evening meal in front of Netflix. If he doesn't find a date for any allocated evening, then he attends a singles night with one of the two dating groups he found within his local area on Meetup.com. These days he spends four or five nights a week in social company, rather than just Saturday and Sunday evenings, and all his colleagues agree that he has become much friendlier to be around now that the spring has returned to his stride. Charlie has once again found balance in his life and he is back in his groove, dreaming of the day that he will one day referee a cup final for the game that he loves.

Chapter Six

Becoming 'proactive' rather than reactive

'Some people want it to happen, some wish it would happen, others make it happen.'

Michael Jordan[71]

In life we have a simple choice - we can either choose to be the pen that writes the script, or become the paper upon which others write theirs. This is not to suggest that we should all strive to become *'alpha'* people and seek to impose our will upon others, or that we should compete with the crowd in an effort to become leaders in our own right. In fact, attempting to join the proverbial 'rat race' is the very antithesis of the reasoning behind this book. Besides, the dire consequences of constructing a society composed entirely of 'alpha' people was eloquently predicted by Aldous Huxley in his dystopian vision 'Brave New World'.[72] We are however *seeking to regain control of our lives and destinies* as far as is possible, although there can be no sureties in a world governed by the forces of nature and humanity. After all, no inventor or entrepreneur would ever have created a venture of worth if they had simply sat and waited for permission before embarking upon their journey. In this chapter we will begin by addressing our *rules of engagement,* and how it is reasonable for us to behave, before considering those courses of action and social constructs which are entirely unreasonable. We will then discuss how we can start to direct our own life program.

---

[71] American basketball legend
[72] 'Brave New World' by Aldous Huxley (1932)

'Every day is a school day.'

The learning curve

Life never ceases to present us with fresh challenges and opportunities from which we can learn. A great proportion of our brain's capacity is dedicated to the processing of events and to the storage of memories, especially those which are the outcomes of our actions and experiences. This is a vital adaptation for our survival, as, if we don't learn from our mistakes, then we will either fail to prosper or cease to exist altogether. We are the collective sum of our decisions – if we make enough good ones then we may thrive, but if we make too many bad judgements, then we set ourselves upon the road to ruin. Wisdom is simply the term we give to life's many accrued lessons.

Our true education is continuous and does not conveniently come to an end as soon as we receive a graduation certificate with a signature – another stamp of social approval. Learning respect and tolerance for other cultures is perhaps more important than any equation or date that may be scrawled on a school chalkboard. While memorizing the names of all the Presidents of the United States or all the capitals of the world may well be an impressive feat of memory - one which has been rendered largely pointless by the advent of mobile phones and search engines - it simply does not help us to simplify the world into a narrative that we can understand, or enable us to navigate towards a place of happiness and contentment.

Many of the world's most successful individuals received little or no formal education. Sir Richard Branson[73] left school at the age of sixteen with no formal qualifications, and many other great visionaries, including Bill Gates[74], Mike Maloney[75], and Mark Zuckerberg[76], all dropped out of college. They were, in a manner of speaking, *'simply too smart for school.'* Those who possess great vision seem to be able to teach themselves what they need to know

---

[73] Founder of the Virgin brand
[74] Co-founder of Microsoft
[75] Mike Maloney, precious metals investor & author of 'The Hidden Secrets of Money'
[76] Co-founder of Facebook

(which has become much easier with the explosion of online content) and have the necessary focus to put into motion the things they need to do to make their vision a reality.

This is not an attempt to cast doubt upon all aspects of our formative education. A basic command of mathematics, language, computing and elementary science are indispensable, although some of us later come to wish that we had brought our formal educations to an end a little earlier than we actually did... Our world is full of bright young minds who mastered the arcane laws of mathematics, law, economics or science, yet find themselves working long hours within poorly paid positions, often in jobs that do not make direct use of such knowledge. We certainly *need* to become specialists in what we do for a living, but should seek to *master our trades* through working experience rather than by taking expensive college courses. To put it another way, we should use our early education to become strong 'generalists' with a good grasp of many subject areas, thereby creating a broad map of our world as a frame of reference, and save the process of specialization for what we eventually come to do for a living.

It could be argued that the greatest teaching method ever devised was that developed by the American Navy in the undue haste of WWII[77]. Under pressure, the US Navy found itself having to quickly train raw recruits to become proficient submariners. Known as *'monkey see, monkey do,'* these young novices were first instructed how to operate a submarine at a practical level, and then later asked to read their manuals to understand what they had learned. Using a similar approach, we can teach ourselves virtually anything we need to know by first cultivating an interest in the subject, and then studying the topic at a practical level. Once we have obtained a grasp of what is entailed, then we can finally proceed towards selective reading to gain a greater level of insight. It is much easier to understand the theory when we can visualise the subject from direct personal experience.

For instance, we might want to know how to take better photographs with a digital camera. However, as we are in our photographic infancy, we are still very much 'stuck on auto', despite our desire to create bolder, sharper and more colourful images. In order to achieve this, we need to understand why camera shutter speeds matter, which lens we should select, and how

---

[77] Second World War, United States involvement from 1941-45

we can make the most of the light that is available to us. All things considered, this is a tricky set of 'variables', and the best way to learn is to change each in turn and view the end results. Once we have gained some practical insight into using a camera, then we can begin to read the various technical explanations and understand why subtle changes in settings can make big differences to the final image. By changing each element in turn, we slowly gain a mastery of the camera and can finally begin to 'paint with light', rather than simply capturing what is in front of us with a click of the button. Through this process we become creative 'artists' rather than merely passive observers. In life we should never stop learning - as the world never ceases to conjure up new challenges. Fortunately, the human brain has the capacity to meet the constant challenge of adapting to changes within our environment. The only real problem we face, is finding the will and *the necessary time* to overcome these obstacles to our progress.

In short, **to cross the gain line** we first have to visualize our goal, determine which milestones we must pass in order to get there, and identify which skills and assets we need to acquire in order to achieve our final objective. This process requires vision, planning, patience, and some focused learning and research. However, there is no need to register for an expensive and time-consuming course to learn everything someone else thinks we need to know about a given subject area. Learning how someone else does something denies us the very opportunity to reason, innovate and explore new ways and means of making our goals become our reality. Remember, if anyone *is truly a master of their craft*, they will usually be busy practicing it and not teaching it... *To learn from the masters*, we have to read their books, study their works, and watch videos of their exploits.

Establishing a code of conduct

Life, in all its many aspects, is about seeking balance. There are very few absolute certainties in this world, although there exist a great many subjective judgements. This need for balance also holds true when we seek to become *'proactive'* rather than *'reactive'* in our approach. We should not simply accept whatever opportunities we are given, or take those lesser paths that are laid out for us in exchange for dutiful compliance and obedience - these are not paths to happiness or fulfilment. Equally we should remember that leaders are chosen by popular acclaim and not self-appointed, and understand that the quickest way to the top of the tree within any enterprise is to plant your own acorn. We make the most gainful advances by improving ourselves and becoming role models through doing so. Accordingly, we must redirect our efforts and attentions inwardly in an effort to become more courteous, efficient and focused, rather than trying to cosmetically improve our external image. A winning smile and a sharp suit may gain a great deal of attention and open many doors, but it is inner substance, rather than superficial style, that ultimately achieves goals and keeps you in good standing.

Although we vary greatly in our means, social backgrounds, educations and personalities, there are nonetheless some common values and standards that we can all reasonably agree upon. The laws of the land are well established and enforced, but there are also many *unwritten rules* of behaviour and widely held *codes of conduct* which serve to preserve the peace and enable us to achieve a relatively peaceful society, even in the midst of great inequality and overpopulation.

The first of these values is, or certainly should be, *unconditional respect*. The age, gender, race, social background or sexual orientation of another individual should be immaterial. All other individuals should be *unconditionally respected*, and no judgements should be made from outward appearances. We all have strengths and weaknesses, and are all vulnerable to the fluctuations of fortune. Just because someone was in the wrong place at the wrong time, crossed the road without looking, or lost their time and money on a fruitless venture, it is no reason to judge them harshly. You never know whether you may find yourself in a similar situation one day. Other than keeping an open mind at all times, in practical terms this means showing the same courtesies to a homeless individual as you would to a millionaire. Giving greater respect to someone who is in a better position to bestow favour or patronage is a reflection of one's own inner nature and integrity rather than a testament of good character.

It is important to *respect the 'space and face' of others* and remember that, the less someone has, the more important their personal dignity may be to them. Even small intrusions into someone's personal space can cause them to feel uncomfortable or to become anxious, especially if they are vulnerable. Develop your peripheral vision so that you can be aware of the presence and movements of others without staring at them directly. The only time you should engage in direct eye contact with another person is if they are talking to you. Allowing your 'eyes to wander', scanning the form and appearance of others, can make them feel uneasy and awkward, as they may sense that you are making uninvited judgements or displaying unwelcome 'interest'. Other than the obsessed and the infatuated, only predators and psychopaths stare intently at others.

The golden rule of *treating others as you would like to be treated* is not simply an ancient wisdom - it also serves as a useful tool for introspection. If we consider how our behaviour might appear to others, then we can learn to behave more considerately to our fellow beings. This simple truth should be self-evident, and it is common sense to realise the consequences of even a few individuals failing to follow a simple social rule or convention. Imagine what would transpire if just a few people started jumping the queue or using their mobile phones in a library. The same principle applies to being timely. Being late for an appointment is immensely disrespectful. Why should someone leave their home or office to be on time for you, when you arrive at the last possible minute? You are merely stating, albeit at a subconscious level, that your time is more valuable than theirs. If you are going to be late, for whatever reason, always apologize profusely in advance as this restores respect.

In any given social situation, we should *always put others first*. If you arrive at a door at the same time as another individual, or if a formal queue has not formed, invite the other persons to go through first. This demonstrates respect and sends the clear message that you do not regard yourself as being more important than others. The same principle applies to the last item of food on a plate, the solitary seat on a train, or the final item in a sale. Fighting or jostling for resources may gain you momentary advantage, but remember that life is ultimately a journey and not a competition, and nobody cares for 'pushy' or overly competitive people. We are as we do, and if we do not prevent ourselves from taking every possible opportunity to be one step ahead, then we inevitably become a reflection of our behaviour. Never push in or 'steal' an opportunity. There is simply no point in creating animosity merely to gain a temporary advantage. Sometimes it is better to lose out on a deal or a cab than to be regarded as the one who prised an opportunity away from another. It is always a better policy to amass good will than to leave disgruntled rivals in your wake. A legacy of ill will always catches up with us eventually.

'Jealousy is all the fun you think someone else had.' - Erica Jong

It is of equal importance to acknowledge the achievements and blessings of others gracefully. Despite our inherent tendency to begrudge the good fortunes of our friends, colleagues and competitors, it is nonetheless a *fundamental law of nature and of mathematics* that it is impossible to distribute the world's resources entirely fairly and equally.[78] This applies to where we live, how much we own, and even our genetic inheritance. It is a simple reality that we do not all work as hard, enjoy the same good weather, or have access to the same resources and opportunities, and there is also the inescapable factor of luck to throw into this heady mix of inequalities. Just as the Dalai Lama warns us to be wary of becoming attached to material possessions, we should also resist the temptation to lapse into jealousy, as such envy distorts our own values and clarity of purpose. How can we ever be contented or happy if we constantly crave the lifestyles and possessions of others, or desire to be somebody else? Contentment could be defined as being comfortable within one's own skin. As the American author Joan Didion once put it, *'to cure jealousy is to see it for what it is, a dissatisfaction with oneself.'*

In seeking a cure for our innate tendency to compare ourselves to others[79], it is perhaps gainful to adopt the habit of always beginning any personal judgement of another group or individual, whether openly or privately, with a positive analysis before engaging in any manner of criticism.

---

[78] Pareto's principle predicts inequalities in terms of distribution. For example, a minority of pods contain the majority of the peas; a minority of 'alpha males' father most of the offspring and, classically; most of the wealth of a nation resides within the hands of a minority of the population.

[79] Despite the fact that self-comparison is a rational frame of reference.

If you note that someone is behaving oddly, start off with a compliment before softly suggesting that their behaviour might otherwise be inadvisable. For instance, if you encounter a group of youths huddled deep in conversation on the sidewalk, blocking access to other pedestrians, engage their attention by first exclaiming, *'It's great to see you guys here!'* Such a positive opening might make them more receptive to your subsequent inference that others might like to be able to pass by. It is gainful to reflect that you have no more right of way on this planet than anyone else, and thus requesting unhindered passage should be a courtesy and not an expectation. We are all a little territorial by nature, but sometimes we have to remind ourselves that we are not always 'top dogs' and do not have a greater right to park on a city street just because we are a resident or property owner.

In the world of office politics, before launching into any criticism of a colleague, begin by going to great lengths to point out their positive attributes prior to passing any judgement upon their shortcomings. For instance, you might say to your assembled colleagues, *'Bob's a great man with a sharp mind, and I particularly like the way he goes to such lengths to prepare his presentations, but I do wish he would be on time.'* Nothing sounds quite as bad (or as unprofessional) to your colleagues as someone 'bad-mouthing' an absent associate. Whether you are casting scathing criticisms within social or professional circles, confidence in you will soon evaporate when you talk negatively or disrespectfully about others behind their back. As a simple rule of personal conduct, impress upon yourself that you will never say anything about someone in their absence that you would not say to their face. This is another essential strand of character development.

We should also accept, other than the law of the land and tacitly accepted codes of conduct, that our personal morality, whether it derives from our culture, religious influence, or reflective philosophy, is ours alone and should not be imposed upon others. Equally, we should always be careful to practice what we preach, as hypocrisy is no virtue and it is only a matter of time before those who are unfaithful to their vows are caught *'in flagrante delicto'*.[80] It is not only crucial that we *'do the right things'* in public, but also that we uphold such standards within our

---

[80] *in flagrante delicto (Latin)* – meaning "caught in the act" or "caught red-handed"

private lives. Character is with us always, even when we are alone, and immoral actions which receive no formal caution or reprimand are dangerously habit-forming. For instance, a civil servant or politician may find that putting personal pleasures 'on their expenses' goes unnoticed initially. However, after a period of good fortune, defrauding the public purse becomes a habit and soon caution turns to carelessness and a full audit of all expenses... Personality is how we behave when others are watching, whereas character is how we conduct ourselves when others are not. Ultimately it is our character that we take with us into the world, and this is what gives us strength and resilience in times of adversity.

Whatever your walk of life, there are usually opportunities to exploit or abuse your position, whether this takes the form of gratuities, sexual gratification, or embezzlement. As always, it is better to avoid the 'perks' of the job, lest they become habitual. Getting away with something is not a moral validation of a behaviour, and colleagues who turn a 'blind eye' are in no way condoning the actions of an errant associate, but rather seeking to avoid the inevitable fallout of being identified as the whistle-blower.

There is of course a code of conduct in all aspects of life, romance and business. Many of these rules, although unwritten, are in place for a good reason – to ensure social harmony within a highly competitive and densely-populated world. While life may at times seem unfair, engaging in fraud, theft, assault or defamation does not solve any problems, and such behaviours only create more turbulence in their wake. Be gentle in your affairs and bear in mind that everyone has feelings and sensitivities - even if they are good at hiding them. The ability to 'sell someone a rejection' is both an art and an invaluable social grace. If you are hiring for a position and reject a candidate, praise their positive attributes and leave them with hope for the future. It is better to suggest that their abilities lie elsewhere, than to inform them that 'their services are not required'. If you have to let someone down in love, in business, or in life, then do so gently and always seek to infer that the failing is your and not theirs.

The problem with social constructs

While many rules and codes of conduct exist which seem entirely sensible for us all to follow, such as patiently waiting in line or paying debts of honour, there are also those social constructs which appear, upon closer examination, to be entirely without basis in law or morality. Some of these are rules of obedience which we have been conditioned to accept, whether through the slick psychology of marketing or by the will of a ruling elite. Whatever the reason for their existence, they are usually very damaging to our social and psychological well-being. Perhaps the most challenging aspect of applying our personal philosophy is in differentiating between those codes of conduct which derive from tradition and culture, and those social constructs which are detrimental to the common good. Once we begin to peer beneath the veneer of our society then such edifices become increasingly self-evident. However, for the purpose of brevity, we shall only focus upon those social constructs which are largely self-evident and impede our personal growth. Once we have removed such 'psychological shackles' then we will be able to move forward more freely with our goals.

'No one can make you feel inferior without your consent.' - Eleanor Roosevelt

Perhaps the most deeply entrenched of all social constructs is the notion that one individual can, by way of some esoteric or arcane convention, automatically assume a higher standing in society than another, and thereby consider themselves 'superior' in terms of their entitlements. Our media and film industries have long fascinated over the rituals of ennoblement and the clandestine ceremonies of the ruling elite, in effect 'validating' their standing. However, we are not intending to discuss the initiation rites of secret societies or to advocate tracing the ancestral trees of powerful families, although we will acknowledge that they exist and wield immense power and influence. While it is essentially true to state, within our complex human social hierarchies, that some individuals either assume or are elected to positions of responsibility which effectively put them in direct authority over others, such power should nevertheless only be confined to specific contexts. For instance, when you enter a doctor's surgery, he or she will automatically assume the lead within the relationship, as the patient essentially assumes a role of deference to the accepted medical authority. Similarly, if you walk down a street and encounter a police officer who is responsible for upholding the law, the officer (regardless of their age, gender or socioeconomic status) is generally accepted to hold a position of authority over you in relation to any interactions which are necessary to maintain public law and order. However, in discharging their responsibilities, police officers are expected to remain courteous and respectful at all times. This principle of *unconditional respect* should hold true for all walks of professional and social life. Alas, as many of us will have experienced, this is often not the case. When we discuss sensitive matters with an accountant or a lawyer, they sometimes adopt a patronising or authoritative air, despite the fact that we are actually paying them. Frequently, when we visit a restaurant, an immaculately dressed waiter may adopt a condescending tone if they sense that we do not conform to the expected 'class' or ambience of their establishment. The list is of course extensive, from our interactions with managers at work to which hotels or clubs we may gain access to.

Despite society's endless reinforcement of its class system, it is essential that you adapt your philosophy to accept the basic premise that you are neither superior, nor inferior to anyone else. No matter where you travel in the world you will encounter a belief system in which others instantly presume themselves to be superior to you by virtue of their personal wealth, the level of their education, or the social clubs they frequent. Although such class systems may be self-perpetuating and ultimately nonsensical, they nonetheless present a minefield of sensibilities which have to be negotiated. We are however able to address this pervasive problem through our acceptance of the *universal law of unconditional respect*, in which we simply agree to treat all others, whether high or low in station, with courtesy and politeness. In more practical terms this means that we do not bow or '*kowtow*'[81] to those who feel themselves superior to us, nor we do tacitly accept their imagined supremacy. In essence this distils down to being firm and polite at all times and in all engagements. When approached with unwelcome instructions or 'suggestions', it is important to be tactful in declining such

---

[81] Kneeling and bowing so low as to have one's head touching the ground as a mark of respect and subjugation.

advances, irrespective of how alluring or inappropriate they may be. For instance, if someone requests that you come and help with an event at the weekend and you have already made other plans, simply respond that you *'would have been pleased to have been able to make a contribution, but regret that you have a prior commitment.'* If a senior colleague or employer requests that you make yourself available for a meeting or 'assignation' outside of normal working hours, simply respond politely that you *'are sorry, but have a previous engagement'*. At this point, their designated 'power' is immediately limited to the confines of the office, an environment in which even their behavioural ambitions are formally constrained.

If someone asks 'what you do' *(for a living)*, merely respond generally and without offering any specific details *(for example state that you are a student, an artist, or 'work in the city')*. If they press further, politely decline to give any additional information as to where you work, were born or were educated, or indeed any other minutiae that would enable them to 'pinpoint' your location, background or socioeconomic status. The ensuing silence may be awkward, but can be simply diffused with a polite smile.

If an employer asks you to do some work that you are not paid to do, or are uncomfortable with, merely respond that you are *'unfamiliar with that task/application, as it was not mentioned within your job specification'*, or request whether they *'would be so kind as to show you how it is done.'* In this way, without actually refusing to comply with their wishes, you place them in a position in which it would take them longer to train you than it would to do it themselves or re-delegate the work to someone else. There is also a more pointed purpose to this repositioning. Once you effectively agree to do hours or services that you are not paid to do, then you place yourself upon a slippery slope in which you will find it increasingly difficult to refuse. As with all such psychological battles, if you concede the first trench without any significant resistance, then you will find that you have already surrendered the last line of defence. Once this happens you will inevitably be overrun until such time as they have availed themselves of all the resources and 'services' they desire from you.

As mentioned, there is also the irrationality that underlies the social construct of 'working hours', a system in which management prefers to measure productivity in terms of the number of hours spent in the workplace rather than monitoring the quality of individual output. In many instances there is little that we can do to change this culture, other than requesting to work from home or part-time. As considered previously, we can at least make the most efficient use of the time that we are bound to spend in the office, by adopting such strategies as batching our tasks and decluttering our schedule. We can also reasonably adapt the lunch hour to schedule our activities outside of office hours and make calls that otherwise cannot be made during the day. However, we will not advocate seeking permission to work from home as a strategy, although this is a good option if made available. Rather the goal should be to reprioritize our lives to ensure that our weekends and evenings become the hub of our productivity and happiness, until such time as we gain sufficient momentum to leave our jobs without precipitating financial fears. In our efforts to appease our employers, one of the worst habits we lapse into is that of *'presenteeism'*, in which we occupy a chair or an office for longer than the prerequisite number of hours simply to be seen to be doing so. Such behaviour is ultimately self-defeating, as it effectively negates any motivation to become goal-orientated or to complete objectives as efficiently and quickly as possible. This echoes Parkinson's Law[82], which asserts that work expands to occupy the time available for its completion. In other words, the social construct of long working hours serves no rational purpose other than as a means of restricting individual liberty.

In a sense, this 'temporal possession' of employees or, in other words, keeping them within the work environment for as long as possible, irrespective of any prevailing employment laws or contracts, could simply be viewed as an extension of the ownership of 'human capital'.[83] It could also be regarded as a more pernicious form of patronage, or even as a rebranding of slavery. However, we can challenge such employment attitudes through our actions, rather than just submitting to the governing will. Remember, everyone has an employer or 'greater entity' to whom they are ultimately answerable, even the President of the United States or the CEO of an international corporation. Declining any unreasonable demands effectively forces the individual making them to either formally acknowledge that they consider you to be a slave

---

[82] 'Parkinson's Law' by C. Northcote Parkinson (1957)
[83] Defined as the knowledge and skills of the human workforce which is capitalised as saleable 'productivity'

or else to retreat for fear of 'overstepping the line'. Given that slavery is still, in principle at least, outlawed, they will rarely dare to enforce their will.

Another irrational social construct is the perceived need to wear expensive suits to work, or otherwise adopt clothes and other fashionable accessories as 'badges' to convey imagined social class. The 'power' of the uniform is undeniable, and an image of an SS officer or German Stormtrooper encapsulates a million words of history. Although it may provide some semblance of reason for a soldier, fireman or a police officer to wear a uniform as a means of identification, it otherwise makes little sense for the average office worker or city employee to follow suit. Yet, many of us are expected to wear 'appropriate' business attire, often at great personal expense, to project our professionalism and dedication to duty. Other than the sheer impracticality of cycling to work in clothes that must be dry-cleaned and kept presentable at all times, they are also ill-suited to public transport, eating, drinking, a rainy day and warm weather. Paradoxically, many offices permit a less formal summer dress code, but if this sacred 'principle' can be dropped for duration of the summer months without risk of damage to a company's reputation, then surely they can be dispensed with all year round, thereby saving a great many of us a small fortune in clothes and dry cleaning bills we would really rather avoid. Many industries, including the IT sector, have already adopted an informal dress code, even wearing jeans and sweaters to work as symbols of defiance. For the rest of us, the best way for us to circumvent such nonsensical conventions is to wear smart casual clothes to the office and make a statement.

Of course there are those social constructs which, although they arise outside of the office environment, are no less frustrating or psychologically damaging. Perhaps the most significant of these social constructs are those 'taboos' which relate to human sexuality and to naturally occurring psychoactive compounds, or 'drugs'.

In relation to the fraught subject of human sexuality, it is a criminal offence (under certain circumstances) to send an image of a human being within their natural state (i.e. naked), to another individual, or even to view or download such images. Sending a naked image of yourself to another individual via a mobile phone is now defined as 'sexting', even in the event that no sexual activity (in terms of 'indecency' or obscenity[84]) has actually arisen. Upon closer reflection, the very notion that the naked, or natural human form is intrinsically obscene is patently ridiculous, although if you were to walk topless in your underwear along a city street on a warm summer's day then you may well risk being cautioned, or even arrested. Other cultures have absolutely no issues or 'hang ups' with public nudity (take for instance, certain African and South American tribes or Scandinavian mixed public saunas), although much of the Western world has created a culture in which the natural human form is prohibited, and even actively censored. Recently, the publication of an advertisement displaying an image of a young woman *in a bikini* caused such outrage on the London Underground, that it led to a formal banning[85] of all such depictions, as much for their presentation of a sexually attractive female form as for their unrealistic representation of the feminine figure. This new wave of sexual prohibition has extended to the much maligned genre of the men's magazine, although curiously not to those publications of male nudity aimed at a female audience.

Similar pervasive social attitudes are extended to the uncomfortable realm of human sexuality. For example, any deviations from 'socially acceptable' sexual behaviour (for instance, a middle-aged man or woman dating a teenager above the 'age of consent'; cohabiting with multiple sexual partners; payment in kind for sexual services; or any overt indication of promiscuous or deviant sexual behaviour) may result in the exclusion of an individual from 'polite society', and even from certain forms of employment. It does not appear to matter whether such behaviour is actually lawful or occurs between consenting adults. The social preference for monogamy through formal legal 'marriage', a state of fidelity which would make us unique among all primates, not only directly contradicts observed human behaviour, but also fosters an unhealthy hidden subculture of brothels, basement clubs, and 'Grindr parties', in which countless thousands seek to evade society's prying eyes as they engage in acts of human sexuality which *'dare not speak their name.'*

---

[84] Unless we choose to define the naked human form as obscene. Please note that we are not discussing depictions of sexual activity or arousal here.
[85] https://www.theguardian.com/media/2016/jun/13/sadiq-khan-moves-to-ban-body-shaming-ads-from-london-transport

The absurdity of such social constructs becomes even more apparent when it comes to drugs[86], where such addictive psychoactive compounds as caffeine[87], amphetamines[88], opiates[89], and alcohol may be consumed relatively freely, and even prescribed by doctors, whereas other naturally occurring psychoactive substances such as heroin, cocaine and cannabis are prohibited to the point at which a prison sentence may be handed down merely for being caught in possession of them. Whether the motivation for such moral (and scientific) duplicity is financial, political, or based upon the motivational effects of the drug in question, this does not preclude questioning the underlying rationale for such arcane prohibition laws, and certainly does not justify waging a costly and unwinnable war on the consumption of such naturally-occurring substances. Madness, after all, can alternatively be defined as *'repeating the same mistakes and expecting a different outcome.'*

However, perhaps the most damaging social construct of our time was the notion that borrowing money was a legitimate path to ownership and thereby individual empowerment. From governments and corporations to families and individuals, the evolution of the entire economic system over the past thirty years has been based upon financing the acquisition of companies, commodities, property, vehicles, educations (and even clothes and entertainment) through debt. Other than challenging the idea that you can truly own anything with money that has been borrowed, it could be argued that we have succeeded in creating a society in which our emotional needs have been diverted towards largely materialistic ends, where buying a new dress or car somehow creates a sense of personal and social fulfilment. The absurdity of persuading a family or an individual that they have actually become a 'home owner' after borrowing hundreds of thousands of dollars or pounds from a financial institution defies all reason. As the late Felix Dennis once mused, the concept of the ownership of any form of property, whether this be a house or shares in a company, through the possession of an electronic or written document is at best a bizarre system.

---

[86] Defined here as any chemical substance administered to the body with the intention to produce a psychological or physiological change in well-being.
[87] As coffee, tea or purified chemical
[88] Including Ritalin, Adderall & Dexedrine.
[89] Including the prescription opiates methadone, Vicodin, OxyContin & Percocet

The premise that everything should be nominally 'owned' by the state, an individual or a corporation, effectively destroys the very idea of 'the commons', a now ancient (and effectively obsolete) term for those natural lands and resources which were once collectively owned by everyone. This wilful creation of a culture of 'commodification', in which *literally anything*, including our fellow human beings, can be formally owned, given a price tag and then sold on for profit, is immensely damaging to any culture which seeks to be humane or to coexist in harmony with nature. Once our society embraced the collective ideal of the commons and our right to free assembly, an era in which street fairs were held frequently and everyone enjoyed the communal 'right of passage' across the land. Today food and drink can only be obtained from commercially licensed bars and restaurants, while street fairs have been rendered all but illegal by bureaucratic red tape. The social and psychological cost of this systemic commodification of society has been the loss of a sense of community, creating in its place an economic order in which the all-consuming individual has become the dominant social entity.

It would of course be unrealistic for us to expect to change this 'reality' within the span of a single generation, but until we come to realise that these phenomena are social constructs rather than the 'natural order' of the world, then we will be unable to redirect our own strategies to achieve a more harmonious and balanced life. The essential realisation is that we should *stop paying for anything with borrowed money*. Debt is the true thief of liberty, in that we effectively become indentured servants to our creditors as soon as we begin to borrow and, as long as we owe money, then we are obligated to take on any form of work at any rate of pay in order to avoid defaulting on our interest payments. In contradiction to the prevailing social logic, renting affords us greater freedom and flexibility than taking on the burden of a mortgage, and the last thing we should ever do is take out a such a gargantuan debt if we ever hope to regain control of our destinies. If you feel that you need to own your own property, then it is better to think small and to save enough money to actually buy one outright, even if this ambition does condemn us to decades of renting.

We have already discussed the antiquated notion that a specialised area of knowledge can only be learned by undertaking a formal course of tuition under the watchful guidance of a respected 'authority' in the field. Such traditional courses are rigorously structured and simultaneously disseminated to hundreds of students at any one time at a cost of tens of thousands per head over a number of years. Now that the Internet has opened up vast vaults of literature, millions of hours of lectures, and countless inspirational videos and documentaries to the masses - entirely free of charge - it would seem irrational that individuals are still willing to sacrifice so many years of their lives to acquire knowledge through an archaic educational system, simply to obtain a signed certificate of validation. Surely the age of the virtual university is now upon us, liberating a new generation from the shackles of a traditional, formalised education? Certainly, the idea of borrowing enormous sums of money simply to attend lectures, write essays, sit examinations and produce original intellectual research for the benefit of the resident academics would seem rather counterproductive.

Our perception of reality is, and always will be, a construct of the mind. We must therefore decide for ourselves what is, and what is not, the 'real truth'. This is why our philosophy is so important, as it enables us to make sense of a world that is becoming ever more volatile and a society that is becoming ever more complex. It is only when we achieve a clear vision and direction that we can start to *reprogram* ourselves to behave in a more thoughtful and more gainful manner. Once we have managed to eliminate many of our less productive activities and have been able to overcome our addition to personal debt, then we can at last begin to make gainful changes to our lives, even if we still hold down a full-time job. In other words, we have to devise strategies which enable us to survive and thrive within an *interdependent* society, and to do this we must first develop a new value system; one which embraces common wisdoms and excludes *(as far as is possible)* social constructs. However, this necessitates a *philosophical 'pole shift'* in which we must *unlearn* much of what we have been programmed to believe - only then can we start to view the world with a fresh perspective.

Chapter Seven

Tools for rescuing time

'My favourite things in life don't cost any money. It's really clear that the most precious resource we all have is time.' - Steve Jobs

If we are to regain control of our lives and achieve a greater balance between work and leisure, it is of paramount importance that we liberate as much of our most precious resource as possible – our *time*. To do this we can adopt three straightforward strategies. These are batching, uncluttering and *'en passant'*.

The importance of batching

No matter how advanced our technological society appears to have become, we always *feel* constrained by those seemingly endless, repetitive tasks which consume so much of our time. For all the labour we may have saved through such innovations as the dishwasher and the microwave, we have simply created other technologies to burn our precious time instead, including automated voice messages, social media and endless Emails.

Whether we are considering trips to the post office or the supermarket, paying bills or ordering groceries online, all such repetitive tasks are best dealt with in bursts, or 'batches'. This applies to countless aspects of our daily lives, from updating our address book to dusting the furniture.

For instance, you may have been invited to many social events over the course of the year and feel obliged to return the favours. However, rather than inviting each set of friends around for dinner in turn, you decide to hold a party and *invite them all*. In doing so, not only do you return their kindness, but you also show them trust by extending one of the most precious gifts of all – the key to your circle of friends and acquaintances. This is also the secret to acquiring and maintaining a close-knit circle of friends, as such an approach enables you to expand your social circle more effectively than would be possible by joining the 'dinner party circuit'. This mode of socialising is also a sincerer form of networking than simply *befriending* people on Facebook, as the empathic communication between two individuals can only occur in the flesh. You only ever get a true feel for the *nature* of another human being when you meet them in person, as all the vital channels of communication are fully open, including their tone of voice, facial expression, body language, and mannerisms.

It is difficult to overcome the behavioural 'imprinting' of the millions of years that it took for us to evolve. As a consequence, despite the relatively recent advent of electronic messages, they still tap into our deep sense of social responsibility to others. Thus we feel obligated to respond as swiftly as possible to all personal communications, regardless of how trivial the topic or unimportant the question. Daily Email exchanges rapidly come to resemble a clumsy chat room, in which all strands of a conversation are repeated over and over again, until a simple sequence of messages requires a search simply to retrieve any kernel of useful information. It is our contention that the best way to approach this very modern dilemma is to respond to your Emails no more than twice a day, condensing all the fragmented messages from the same sender into a single coherent communication. Not only does such batching save a great deal of time, but many superfluous requests and spontaneous questions will have long since resolved themselves by the time you sit down to compose a reply. Besides, if it's truly urgent, they'll call - that's what phones are for. Any individual who regards you as being at their 'beck and call' clearly has no respect for either your time or your schedule, and so you shouldn't feel that you have let them down simply because you haven't responded instantly to an electronic communication which commands you to undertake an 'urgent' task or attend a meeting with little prior notice. If they were more courteous and organised in the first place, then they would have afforded you a reasonable period of notice.

Shopping is one the most effective ways of dissipating time and money, especially if we are taking a stroll through a shopping centre without a specific purchase in mind. While this can be immensely pleasurable, especially if it is for a favourite hobby or pastime, it is usually an otherwise unproductive way to spend a morning or an afternoon. If we choose to view shopping as a 'maintenance activity' (i.e. something we do just to maintain our *status quo*), then we may reason that we should make as few forays to the supermarket, hardware store or mall as possible in order to save time and money.

We can save yet more time if we adopt the habit of freezing half the week's provisions and plan our meals for the coming week rather than continuing to shop at the supermarket on impulse. Even fresh bread can be frozen, and it is far more efficient to cook many portions than it is to prepare just one or two. Economies of scale and effort apply as much to shopping and cooking as to any other process, and it is surprising just how much we do save when we buy and cook in bulk. Once we factor in dining out and eating pre-cooked food, we can limit food preparation to two or three hours a week and also make a sizeable dent in the household budget.

This straightforward principle of batching soon becomes a habit, one which can be applied to all manner of repetitive and time-consuming tasks. Significant amounts of time can be recovered if you only visit the bank or post office once every few weeks and take care of all your business in one sweep. Many small trips burn time (and gasoline) very effectively. Without any risk of exaggeration, batching can free up some two to three hours a day which can be redirected towards more interesting and constructive pursuits in our mission to cross the gain line.

'It is indeed difficult to convey simplicity.' – Bruce Lee

'En passant'

Another key habit to assimilate is that of performing tasks *'en passant'*, or 'in passing' - thereby avoiding the penalties of procrastination. This simply means that we pop into to the store as we are passing rather than making an extra trip, and that we acquire items that we have long intended to buy as and when the opportunity presents itself, rather than turning such acquisitions into a fully-fledged mission. For instance, imagine that you have been keeping an eye out for a new briefcase with a special compartment for a laptop, or that you have wanted to buy a candlestick to give your parents as an anniversary present. Such items can be very difficult to track down, especially in a big city, and almost impossible to assess in terms of size and quality from an image on the Internet. However, *'fortune favours the prepared mind'* as they say, and it is surprising just how frequently we stumble upon what we were looking for, often when we least expect it. Such is the nature of serendipity.

The same principle applies to cleaning. Rather than sacrificing a morning or afternoon every week to make your home more habitable, why not simply 'tidy as you go'? Instead of ignoring messes, clean them up as you pass them by – this is better than leaving them for a draining ordeal at the weekend. Why not puff up and rearrange the cushions and straighten the items on the coffee table as you walk through the living room, rather than frantically rushing around the house ten minutes before your visitors are due to arrive? Soon your weekend deep clean will be reduced to pushing the vacuum cleaner around and a light dusting, freeing up yet more time and energy for what truly motivates you.

Uncluttering your life

Our lives are full of clutter. This is something we soon come to realise when we move house or change jobs. It never ceases to amaze, just how many of the contacts we amass during our travels we are reluctant to move across to a new mobile phone or forward our new address to. When the removals van arrives, it does not have the capacity to accommodate the sheer number of items we bought for occasional use or to occupy a spare corner. Moving house or apartment forces us to take stock of just how much unnecessary 'stuff' we accumulate during the course of our lives; clutter which we then have to purge from our wardrobes, cupboards and spare rooms. We should apply the same cleansing logic to our daily and weekly schedules as we tend to accumulate bad habits and adopt a set of displacement activities[90] simply to kill a spare hour or two and avoid facing the inevitable… We often engage in such behaviours, as playing video games or watching TV seems preferable to facing an unresolved issue or beginning a new project or venture.

Such displacement activities come in many shapes and forms; for instance, browsing catalogues, surfing the Internet, or simply rearranging the items on a desk. If we engage in such patterns of behaviour it is often because we are feeling tired, depressed or listless - all symptoms of a deeply unsatisfying existence. If your day has subsided into a routine of the same commute, dining patterns, and late night light entertainment, then the chances are that your life has become rather stale and that the daily grind of the *'eight to late'* has become a pattern of survival rather than a road towards redemption. If this has a familiar ring to it then, more likely than not, you are less than happy with your world and do not really feel that you are occupying your days gainfully. We all have a purpose in life that goes beyond simply pleasing others or ensuring that the bills are paid. If we are fortunate to discover what truly motivates us then, not only will our days seem shorter and happier, but our productivity will also improve, along with the likelihood of having satisfied colleagues and clients.

Our ideal vocation may elude us for many years until that chance experience or discovery triggers that elusive 'eureka' moment. This may occur during a well-earned holiday or when we

---

[90] Any unnecessary activity that we undertake to avoid doing a more difficult or unpleasant one.

seek a new activity. This moment of realisation can be greatly hastened if we constantly seek to 'freshen the menu' and try new things. If you have yet to find your true calling then, instead of spending your spare evenings and weekends on the couch or in front of a monitor, why not join a few Meetup[91] groups and explore some new hobbies and pastimes that take your fancy? It may be that your true calling is as an artist or writer, but the truth is that you will never know until you try, and sometimes even a dead end can lead to new realisations and friendships.

The process of uncluttering your life should be extended to all aspects of your world and routine, from the endless acquisition of possessions to 'collecting friends' on social media. It is simply not a good use of time or money to buy clothes or kitchenware for all conceivable occasions, and sometimes it makes more sense to rent or hire, as the cost of storage is rarely considered. After all, space is becoming an ever more valuable commodity within an increasingly crowded world.

The advent of modern technology has greatly facilitated our ability to waste time. An endless offering of films, serialisations, games and social media has arisen to tempt our easily distracted minds, and it takes more discipline and clarity of thought than ever to remain focused and 'on mission'. Even within the workplace, new software appears every year to 'streamline' our activities and generate more data for someone to process. Despite the advent of the digital age, the average number of hours we work a week increased from 39 in 1980[92] to over 49 in 2013[93]. While there may be lies, damned lies and statistics, we should note that, for all technology has to offer, our weekly workload is actually increasing.

The principle of uncluttering is as profoundly important to our 'virtual' life as it is to our worldly one. When it comes to friends and contacts on the Internet, unless you are marketing a business, the fewer the better. Hundreds of friends commenting positively upon your social media posts can be flattering, and there is certainly a little 'diva' in all of us that craves attention and adulation. However, the social media experience can quickly turn sour when we are hacked or attacked by an interloper, or receive a hostile broadside in response to a post or

[91] Meetup.com
[92] https://www.minneapolisfed.org/research/qr/qr2812.pdf
[93] http://comptroller.nyc.gov/wp-content/uploads/documents/Longest_Work_Weeks_March_2015.pdf

comment made in innocence. Digital drama aside, we should ask ourselves if we really have the time to read countless posts and respond to communications from hundreds of contacts on a variety of different social media platforms? Are all of these contacts true friends with positive motives? Can we really maintain our privacy online, given the information we inadvertently give away about our favourite haunts, closest friends, and way of life through our many images and posts online? Other than the obvious embarrassment of having to explain an errant kiss, a careless remark, or a drunken antic to an employer, colleague or loved one, it seems highly improbable that all the friends we readily accumulate through social media will turn out to be considerate friends, useful allies, or potentially gainful contacts. Are you really able to find the time to respond to all of their invitations and 'opportunities'? It would seem unlikely.

Every contact on social media is a potential opportunity that requires an investment of time. We do not have to accept many friend requests for it to become a full-time distraction to the detriment of both our professional and personal environments. One of the best places to start the process of uncluttering our lives is a purge of acquaintances on social media sites. Don't worry, they won't be directly informed and, if they ask why they were unfriended, simply state that you have reduced your network to close personal friends only.

Not so many moons ago, a few years before the creation of Facebook, Snapchat and Instagram, the most common way to meet new people and expand your social circle was through the formal process of introductions from trusted friends and colleagues. Less than a generation has passed since the dawn of Facebook and now, all that is required to grant universal access to your personal privacy and peace of mind, is a careless tap of the finger...

One simple and rather effective way of approaching this question is to perform the *quadrant exercise*, in which you put all of your weekly activities into one of four corners which are segregated by means of a cross. This simple exercise enables you to segregate and categorise your activities according to their priority and usefulness.

Walk the dog *Call Sam* *Send minutes to Ralf* *Book service for car* *Buy groceries*	*Learn how to use Photoshop* *Research prime lenses* *Search for online marketing* *course*
Pay gas bill *Cut new door key* *Process images* *Dog food*	*Check out new movie releases* *Surf Instagram* *Shop for new T-shirts* *Share cartoon on Facebook*

In the *top-left quadrant* you list your inescapable priorities; within the *bottom-left quadrant* you jot down those important things that you will need to do fairly soon. In the *top-right quadrant* you can compartmentalise those activities which *you will need to engage with in order to achieve your goals and develop new skills.* Last, and certainly least, fill the *lower-right quadrant* with those activities that have no urgency or gainful purpose. Now simply draw a line through them. You will have no constructive purpose for these, unless you really do want to be trapped within the endless mire of unproductive occupation.

Once you have begun to successfully unclutter your life, have batched all of your repetitive activities, and picked up the habit of attending to errands as you are passing by, then you will have recovered many hours of lost time which you will be able to 'repurpose' to transform your life and **cross the gain line.**

Chapter Eight

The simplifying reason of Mike Mentzer

'In order to lead the orchestra, you must first turn your back to the crowd.'

Mike Mentzer

Mike Mentzer was a remarkable man in many ways - an individual who transcended his chosen walk of life through his empowering philosophy. Mr Mentzer was a man who acted on considered judgement rather than on impulse; a sage who was far more likely to follow his own intuition than the crowd. What he accomplished, within his own field of endeavour, was to successfully challenge the orthodoxy of his time and still prevail. He achieved this transformation through his own philosophical thought process and reasoning and, rather than subscribing to the highly questionable school of thought which dominated his era, he sought a simpler and more effective solution.

Another unsung sophist of the 20th Century, Mike Mentzer left the legacy of a simplifying perspective in his quest for a quietly rational and effective alternative to the repetitive and redundant rituals of the modern world. Perhaps the single most important lesson to be learned from this gentle giant, is an understanding of the transformative power of a rational philosophy when applied to a given task or objective.

A former student of genetics and organic chemistry, Mike Mentzer went on to serve for four years within the United States Air Force. During his period of service, he developed a fascination for bodybuilding and began training in accordance with the prevailing school of thought of his era – undertaking arduous three hour workouts every day, seven days a week. Eventually, after being side-lined for many years with a serious shoulder injury[94] and suffering the frustrations of defeat in his early contests, he later resumed training with a revised ideology and ultimately went on to become a heavyweight champion of the late seventies. In 1980 he retired abruptly at the age of 29 after losing to

---

[94] He suffered in 1971

Arnold Schwarzenegger, but what distinguished him from his contemporaries was his holistic philosophical approach to life which he regarded as his 'art'.

From years of patient study, thoughtful observation, and a detailed comprehension of the science of muscle and stress physiology Mike Mentzer created, tried and tested his own theory of bodybuilding, rejecting the 'law of more' that was officially advocated by the contemporary ruling elite. Mike Mentzer was truly a black swan of his era.

In actual fact, Mr Mentzer's pioneering principle was intentionally devised to help all athletes and fitness fanatics to achieve their full potential within a short timeframe, simply by increasing the intensity and decreasing the volume and duration of their workouts. He reasoned that muscles increase in size and strength primarily because they are subjected to a sudden and extreme *stress*, rather than in response to *exhaustion*. He deduced that athletic training had to be short, sharp, infrequent and intense to obtain swift and gainful results, because muscles had to recover before they could grow. Therefore, according to his unassailable logic, the vast volumes of training advocated by his contemporaries were extremely counterproductive. To quote the clear and lucid reasoning of Mike Mentzer, *'You must understand that the workout does not actually produce muscular growth. The workout is merely a trigger that sets the body's growth mechanism into motion. It is the body itself, of course, that produces growth; but it does so only during a sufficient rest period.'* Thus Mike Mentzer revolutionised the world of athletic training, and his once radical ideas eventually became embedded within mainstream thinking.[95]

By choosing to remember his contributions as a mentor and a philosopher (rather than as a bodybuilding champion), Mike Mentzer has yet more to teach us in terms of the rational simplification of our approach to any aspect or challenge within our lives. Mike Mentzer simply would not advocate doing anything in a more complex or time-consuming manner than is absolutely necessary, and he applied his 'objectivist'[96] philosophy to all aspects of his storied life. In a nutshell, the objectivist school of reason argues that we interact with 'reality' through our senses and can acquire 'objective knowledge' from perception by understanding concepts and subjecting them to logical scrutiny. Notably, objectivists believe that the rightful moral purpose of our lives is ultimately the pursuit of happiness (which they call *'rational self-interest'*), and that this requires a social and political system which enshrines individual human rights.

---

[95] 'The Wisdom of Mike Mentzer: The Art, Science and Philosophy of a Bodybuilding Legend' John R. Little, 2005
[96] A philosophical school of thought originally devised by author Ayn Rand.

In keeping with the spirit of the preceding chapters, Mike Mentzer would also have championed thought before action, given that he taught, *'It is only within the context of having properly developed your mind that you will be able to truly enjoy the achievement of your material values.'* In other words, only a cultivated mind can enjoy the fruits of its labours. To put it in simpler terms, we are unable to appreciate anything that we have not worked towards, as we are unable to value the true cost of its acquisition, or what has been sacrificed to achieve our goals.

Mike Mentzer specifically emphasised the importance of the ideation and visualisation of goals as a prerequisite to attaining them. To put this concept in his own words, *'One cannot actualize one's goals until one visualizes them clearly in the mind's eye.'*

Just as importantly, Mike Mentzer, like our next philosopher, realised that any additional time, resources or effort which are expended, above and beyond what is actually required to achieve an end goal, is simply wasteful. However, as we are socially conditioned to believe that we are measured - and hence valued - in terms of the number of hours of selfless service that we dedicate to our labours (rather than by the productive outcome of our endeavours) we continue to push ourselves beyond the call of duty. We shall though leave the final words of wisdom to Mike Mentzer, *'Any activity carried on beyond the least amount required to stimulate an optimal gain is not merely a waste of effort, it is actually highly counterproductive.'*

Chapter Nine

The wisdom of water

'Have no way as way, and no limitation as limitation.' - Bruce Lee

Most famous people are remembered for what we see them do, rather than for the thoughts and actions that truly define them. For instance, we see Angelina Jolie and George Clooney as famous actors rather than as great humanitarians; we associate Gisele Bündchen and Alicia Keys with glamourous lifestyles *(when in fact they donate a great deal of their time and money to charitable causes)*; and we revere Bruce Lee solely for his prowess as a martial artist. It was however as a philosopher that Bruce Lee left his greatest legacy. His singular approach to refining his method to the height of simplicity and efficiency could be viewed as a form of minimalism[97], while his emphasis on the importance of fluidity and flexibility in movement, mind and method provide us with a complete *'tao'*, or *'way'* through which we can navigate the complexities of the Western world in our search for that peace of mind which can only come from balance.

Life and living systems ebb and flow like water. If we can learn to view life and the natural world surrounding us as being fundamentally cyclical, then we can learn to live in harmony with nature. The cyclical nature of life is evident everywhere we look, from the phases of the moon to the length of day, to the seasons and their rhythmic abundance and disappearance of life and its myriad colours. For us to survive and thrive we *must adapt to these cycles* rather than constantly seeking to resist them. To do so offers great advantage.

---

[97] Minimalism is a school with seeks to engender freedom from the consumer culture, the expectations of social constructs and materialism. http://www.theminimalists.com/

In relation to our own individual cycles; when we feel tired we should seek to rest; when we are inspired we should move ourselves to act; and when we are afforded rare opportunity, then we should make the most of it. The same philosophy applies to our harmony with nature. When we are in the summer season we should make the most of its fruits, and when in the midst of winter, we should aim to consolidate and lay the groundwork for the forthcoming cycle of opportunity. We have to learn to sense the flow of the world around us in order to avoid hazards and sense advantage. We have to learn to exist in harmony with our surroundings and not to resist those energies and forces that do not favour our advancement or advantage. As Bruce Lee would put it;

> *'Art is the way to the absolute and to the essence of human life. The aim of art is not the one-sided promotion of spirit, soul and senses, but the opening of all human capacities – thought, feeling, will – to the life rhythm of the world of nature. So will the voiceless voice be heard and the self be brought into harmony with it.'*

The wisdom of water

As a man of great perspicacity, Bruce Lee advocated that we should learn to behave like water, to flow around obstacles rather than to confront them, and to be flexible and durable in our approach to life. He argued that while water may appear 'soft' in its form, it is indestructible, able to withstand the elements and, through its persistence, even reduce rock to rubble. Like water, we need to flow within our surroundings, to adapt to the moment, and to move through every opening presented. This sense of timing is critical to our survival and success in life as it is in nature. We should not make our move, or invest our time, energy and resources, until the opportunity presents itself to our prepared minds and resources. It is always inadvisable to take a positive action until the time is right and we are prepared to exploit and consolidate any opportunity.

'There is a tide in the affairs of men, which, if taken at its height, leads on to fortune.' – William Shakespeare[98]

The themes of water and balance with our surroundings dominated his thinking, and Bruce Lee saw all life as essentially being in a constant state of flux and our fortunes as continuously flowing.

> *'Flowing in the living moment, as we are always in a process of becoming and nothing is fixed. It is unwise to adopt or apply any rigid system in your methods, as this affords flexibility to the constant changes we face. Open yourself to opportunity and flow. Flow in the total openness of the living moment. When moving, be like water.'* [99]†

In terms of the 'personality' with which we approach life, Bruce Lee suggested that we should constantly adapt to and evolve with our surroundings, rather than straining to adopt a uniform persona in response to all eventualities. In his own words, *'When one has reached maturity in one's art, one will have a formless form. It is like ice dissolving in water. When one has no form, one can be all forms; when one has no style, one can adapt to any situation.'* Through such an approach it is possible to become more receptive - and hence adaptable - to very different situations *(for example relaxing at an office party, or becoming more formal at a business meeting with strangers).* By constantly adapting and responding to our surroundings - and not seeking to impose our will or way upon others - we are in a better position to encourage opinions and events to flow in our favour. In his words,

> *'One should be in harmony with, not in opposition to, the strength and force of the opposition. This means that one should do nothing that is not natural or spontaneous; the important thing is not to strain in any way.'*

---

[98] Julius Caesar: Act 4, Scene 3
[99] † His quotations have been abridged and paraphrased to ensure contemporary relevance in context.

This concept of flexibility and adaptability pervades his philosophy. Bruce Lee understood that our lives are a constantly changing journey through time, and that we should thus evolve continuously in response to our surroundings. *'Life is never stagnation. It is constant movement, un-rhythmic movement, as we as constantly change. Things live by moving and gaining in strength as they go.'*

His philosophy would have been in broad agreement with that of the new emerging school of minimalism[100] as Bruce Lee realised, through his art and his life, that simplicity is *'the key to brilliance.'* He believed that it is only through the constant refinement and streamlining of our methods that we can achieve excellence and efficiency, and even the slightest deviation - when repeated a thousand times - is a waste of time and energy. As the late master advocated, *'The less effort, the more efficient and effective you will become.'*

'As you think, so shall you become' – Bruce Lee

The importance of motive and motivation

Bruce Lee also believed that the visualisation of our goals is the key to their ultimate success. Such ideation is paramount, not only in attaining our goals, but also in ensuring that we do not become fixated upon and entrapped by material possessions rather than goals and experiences. He saw our ideations as self-fulfilling prophesies, as, *'the spirit of the individual is determined by his dominating thought habits, and what we habitually think largely determines what we will ultimately become.'*

In terms of our goals, Bruce Lee saw our aspirations as a journey rather than as an end in of themselves, as self-improvement is an endless process. In his own words, *'A goal is not always meant to be reached, it often serves simply as something to aim at. If you always put a limit on everything you do - physical or anything else - it will spread into your work and into your life.*

---

[100] http://www.theminimalists.com

There are no limits. There are only plateaus, and you must not stay there, you must go beyond them.'

In life, Bruce Lee was an inherently cheerful individual, who felt that we should always, *'choose the positive. You have choice, you are master of your attitude, choose the positive, the constructive. Optimism is a faith that leads to success.'* In terms of our personal development, he argued that the only true frame of reference is ourselves and hence, *'the function and duty of a quality human being is the sincere and honest development of one's potential.'*

> *'Life itself is your teacher, and you are in a state of constant learning.'*

On learning and personal development

It would come as no surprise to learn that Mr Lee was highly individualistic and, like Mike Mentzer, believed in achieving self-fulfilment through a process of the rational refinement of one's own goals and behaviours, and not simply by adopting the common consensus in terms of our behaviour and actions. As he succinctly put it, *'I'm not in this world to live up to your expectations and you're not in this world to live up to mine.'* Bruce Lee duly cautioned that we should, *'always be ourselves, express ourselves, and have faith in ourselves,'* and that we should, *'not go out and look for a successful personality and seek to duplicate it.'*

With respect to the learning process he offered many valuable insights, and none was perhaps more important than acknowledging that we become our own greatest teachers through the process of reflecting upon the outcomes of our own trials and tribulations.

> *'When there is freedom from mechanical conditioning, there is simplicity. The classical man is just a bundle of routines, ideas and traditions. If you follow the classical pattern, you are understanding the routine, the tradition, the shadow – you are not understanding yourself.'*

In consideration of the spectre of *'failure'* - always a stressful and time-consuming issue, especially in a world with ever greater pressures to succeed - it may be worth reflecting upon a sentiment that has been echoed by many great businessmen and entrepreneurs over the centuries. Bruce Lee captures the essence of their spirit in his own inimitable style, *'do not fear failure. It is not failure we should fear, but rather aiming low. Underachievement is the crime. In great attempts it is glorious sometimes even to fail.'* Sir Richard Branson, Donald Trump and Sir James Dyson[101] would doubtless agree - all individuals who triumphed despite major setbacks and adversity.

Bruce Lee explained concisely how the process of continuous refinement and learning takes place. *'I am not teaching you anything. I am just helping you to explore yourself. You should absorb what is useful, and discard what is not. Add what is uniquely your own. It is not the daily increase but daily decrease that truly matters. Hack away at the unessential.'*

Bruce Lee realised that, despite our great potential as human beings and individuals[102], that, *'the biggest adversary in our lives is ourselves. We are what we become, in a sense, because of the dominating thoughts which we allow to gather in our heads. All concepts of self-improvement, and all actions and paths that we take, relate solely to our abstract image of ourselves. Life is thus only limited by how we really see ourselves and feel about ourselves. A great deal of pure self-knowledge and inner understanding allows us to lay the all-important foundations for the structure of our lives, and it is from these foundations that we can perceive and take the right avenues in life.'*

'If you truly love life, then don't waste time, for life is only lived for a finite time.'

---

[101] An engineer & entrepreneur whose fifteen years of failures led to his reinvention of the vacuum cleaner and many other products since.
[102] Bruce Lee acknowledged that he himself had been a slow learner of 'wing chun' kung fu and also in his school studies.

The importance of time

Above all else, Bruce Lee understood the fundamental importance of time as our greatest and most truly irreplaceable asset. *'To spend time is to pass it in a specified manner. To waste time is to expend it thoughtlessly or carelessly. We all have time to spend or waste, and it is our decision what to do with it. But once passed, it is gone forever.'*

However, he also realised that life is a continuous series of moments, in that we are connected to the past only through our memories, and to our future journey only by our present. *'The moment is a timeless moment. It has no yesterday or tomorrow. It is not the result of thought and therefore has no time. The moment is our precious freedom. Don't live by a rigid schedule. Try to live freely from moment to moment, letting things happen and adjusting to them like water adapting to its vessel.'*

Overlooking his renown as a martial artist and status as an iconic film star, Bruce Lee's greatest legacy was perhaps his unique philosophy, one which continues to challenge Western ideology to this day. Although much of his thinking appears highly antithetical and anachronistic to modern Western culture, we should remember that the late master arrived in America as a teenager and, by the time of his death in 1973 (at the age of 32), he had already become a major movie star, inspiring a global generation from Hong Kong to Hollywood. Regardless of his fame and achievements, there can be no doubt that he has left us much to reflect upon.

Chapter Ten

The principles of strategy and momentum

We do not of course live in a utopian society. The world we inhabit is not populated solely by benign individuals, while nature can, at its worst, be brutal. There are those who would willingly prey upon the energies and opportunities of others, and many more who would swiftly seize or despoil that which others have worked so hard to achieve. To attain peace and prosperity we must be receptive and responsive to gainful opportunities, while remaining 'mindful' of potential threats, both seen and unseen. There is no more tragic waste of a life than someone who locks themselves away from the world, simply due to a fear of failure. Again, it is a matter of balance, and we should be prepared to face potential challenges and competition from others without devoting too much of our precious time and mental energies to defence.

Within this chapter we shall explore the importance of strategy and momentum in achieving our goals and maintaining our essential security. While some of the defensive strategies discussed may at first seem original, much is adapted or cited directly from the annals of ancient wisdom; wisdom which remains as true today as it has ever been. In life, as well as in love, we have to protect that we which value most, including the lives of our loved ones and our most precious possessions.

However, we will not be advocating psychological warfare or the need to take up a martial art, but rather that you learn to develop those psychological defences which increase your chances of surviving and thriving within a competitive and often hostile world. The techniques, strategies and philosophies described below are intended to be simple and consistent with the preceding values of integrity, honesty and fairness in all our dealings.

What your rival doesn't know can't hurt you

In life, many of those who covet our success and happiness don't usually declare their hostility - indeed some are to be found within our most intimate circles. It is therefore pointless to be open and uninhibited with our closest friends and more guarded with casual acquaintances and colleagues. This is simply because those who can do us the greatest harm are those who are closest to us. It is however counterproductive to become paranoid or to start worrying who, within our inner circle, is a true friend and who is a 'frenemy'[103], to employ a popular American term. It is far less stressful to adopt a set of rules of engagement as to how we conduct ourselves socially.

It is however important to be guarded in what we say, especially within a group situation or on social media. There have been many cautionary tales of those who fell into dangerous company through connections they made on social media, and many more of those who had their homes ransacked due to open online party invitations. Perhaps of greater concern though, is the ease with which someone can draw a detailed personal profile of another individual by carefully studying their social media profiles and associated imagery, even if their privacy settings are set to 'friends only'.

For instance, an individual's favourite haunts quickly become apparent - even what days or evenings they frequent them on. An interested party can determine where (or when) someone is going away on holiday, and who their closest friends are, simply by studying the tagged images on a social media profile. It does not take too long to profile someone in alarming detail; including where they work, who their closest friends and colleagues are, and which part of the world they live in. As for other personality profiling characteristics, such as which films, sports, foods and drinks an individual is partial to, these are usually declared without so much as a pause for thought. Thus it would not be very difficult for a predator or adversary to track us down... As a rule of thumb, avoid tagging images, and discuss only where you have been and

---

[103] An enemy who pretends to be a close friend or a friend who harbours an active rivalry.

not where you are going, detailing only where you are from and not where you currently live or work. Self-defence is common sense.

Refrain from 'badmouthing' others, whether you are online or in general company - especially colleagues or employers. You will be surprised just how often your words are disseminated and how many people will actually use their camera phones to record sound or video surreptitiously. In life, as on social media, only talk generally and not specifically and, if you do feel the urge to participate in the 'white noise' of Twitter, Facebook and Instagram, restrict yourself to only making broad comments and to being as positive about others as possible. Specific statements, especially those which are negative, only assist others to associate us with unhelpful stereotypes, for instance that we are sexist, prejudiced, ignorant, promiscuous or 'liberal' in our behaviours. Such statements as, *'Great barbeque Dan, thank you for a wonderful evening!'*, or *'Good to see you!'* are both positive and innocuous, and do not leave us unduly exposed to unwarranted criticism. In a world where opinions count for so much, it is unwise to speak too freely or to publish thoughtless remarks for the world to take out of context.

Information is power, and power is influence. Power and influence are readily wielded by those who know how to use them to make money or exert their will. We only have to look as far as big government, or Google and Facebook to see that this is a fundamental truth. However, information is only as powerful as it is accurate, and it is fairly simple to develop a defensive shield that is as effective as it is liberating. We can create this shield by implementing a simple set of rules for our social conduct (both online and offline).

(i)   When in general company or online, only use a nickname or *alter ego* such as a pen name or *'nom de voyage'*. For example, your name may be Samuel Jones, although your close friends and family call you Sammy, or 'Easy Rider', due to your fondness for motorcycles. So your online persona could be 'Sam Rider' or 'Sammy J'. This creates at least a level of difficulty for those seeking to track you down on social media and, when combined with the use of only broad or general statements, helps to makes your online experience altogether safer and more pleasant.

(ii)   Always refrain from expressing strong views in public or on social media. Most people do not know you well, and even fewer can relate to those personal experiences which influence your beliefs and attitudes. Thus strong opinions can be very damaging if they are presented in mixed company, or if your employers and adversaries receive wind of them. Remember, once published online, a photo or remark can never be retracted – even on Snapchat[104].

(iii)   White noise is a powerful defence. For those highly expressive and sociable individuals amongst you who find silence all too constraining, there is something far more effective than silence - an avalanche of information which contains little or no substantial content of useful value to those seeking valuable insight into your nature. For instance, constant chatter about the weather, recipes and good places to eat or visit - as well as endless responses to quizzes and requests to rate place and products – offers those with unhealthy motives a mountain of useless data to mine while keeping your friends and loved ones positively engaged.

(iv)   Never underestimate the power of obfuscation[105]. When it comes to a specific question, the best response is usually an evasive or a non-committal answer. For example, if someone wants to know your holiday plans, simply recount half a dozen places you have been actively considering and the merits of each in turn *(and preferably do not include your intended destination)*. If someone enquires whether you intend to change jobs, merely suggest that you are generally happy where you are and are well-treated, but would actively consider working elsewhere if a suitable opportunity arose. If you are asked how you are feeling or 'how things are going', simply respond that all is well but could always be better. The intent is not to lie or wilfully mislead, but rather to avoid giving specific information away needlessly. For instance, if someone knew that you were having financial difficulties or that there were problems in your marriage, then that would present an invitation to probe for further weaknesses during a period of instability or weakness. If a rival colleague

---

[104] e.g. Hackers get their hands on 100K 'deleted' Snapchat images.
http://www.foxnews.com/tech/2014/10/12/hackers-eye-release-100k-deleted-snapchat-images.html
[105] To make obscure, unclear or confusing through the provision of additional or unnecessary information.

knew that you had to be away from the office due to urgent family problems, then this would present an ideal opportunity to cause a surge in workload so that there would be greater pressure to be in the office outside of normal working hours. Again the goal is not to lie or to deceive, but merely to evade, rather like a squid leaving a smokescreen of ink in its wake that would only bother a predator or someone with an 'unhealthy interest' in your affairs. If someone wants to know who you are dating, other than the obvious reply that it is none of their concern, simply respond that you are 'going out with a friend'.

(v) Follow the old adage of asking all the right questions and not answering any. Information is power, and the world is rife with competition for opportunity and resources. The simplest way for a rival to thwart your plans is for them to know what they are. Never divulge your plans or objectives until they have been realised and cannot be undone. Never underestimate the danger that stems from the self-interest of others, or how far or deep their extended grapevine may be. Only reveal information on a 'need to know basis' and be careful to whom it is disseminated. For instance, imagine you have devised a business strategy which you feel is quite innovative. When pressed by rivals or colleagues for further insight, simply state that you were *'thinking along the lines'* of plan A or B. This is of course undoubtedly true, as you would have actively considered such possibilities before settling upon plan C. If anyone then attempts to disrupt plan A or B by targeting those likely to be in the chain of supply or communication, then they will simply be wasting their time and effort, as your energies will be actively expended upon executing plan C without fear of interception. Most importantly, by only suggesting that you had *actively considered* plan A or B, nobody can infer that you had lied to them. The creation of such *'ghost targets' (whether these are casual acquaintances whom people incorrectly assume you are dating; business ventures that never become anything other than online prototypes; or bars or clubs that you once visited on a Friday night and have never returned to since)* all serve as useful distractions to distract potential adversaries.

(vi)   Keep your enemies guessing. The dissemination of specific information, no matter how innocuous or innocent it may at first appear, can be used to thwart, frustrate or harm your efforts to transform your life. A careless remark may be taken out of context and turned against you; a show of intimate affection to another individual may be misrepresented as an act of infidelity; and any statement of intent offers precise coordinates for an attack or interception. If it is our intention to avoid conflict and disappointment, *'remember what peace there may be in silence'*. Conflict invariably causes us to waste time, energy and resources, and thus avoiding it in all its forms should be a primary objective.

(vii)   We should seek to become the masters of our own destinies. Therefore, we should seek to dance to our own tune and not to those of others. If you serve the whims and wishes of others, you are unlikely to ever find inner peace or contentment. The emancipation of self through the exercise of independent will and deliberative thought is a precursor to being able to pursue one's own goals, *even if this freedom is initially limited to your evenings and weekends.*

The wisdom of Sun Tzu

'The supreme art of war is to subdue the enemy without fighting.' - Sun Tzu

The preceding paragraphs are essentially little more than ancient wisdom reframed within a modern context. Although the ancient Chinese general Sun Tzu may have been famed for his strategic vision, there is nonetheless much wisdom embedded within his classic work *'The Art of War'* which helps us to deal with adversarial situations, although there is little actual discussion of the details of combat. This is probably why the book has stood the test of time, as it relates to the philosophy and strategy of warfare rather than to the ever changing nature of the battlefield. *'The Art of War'* also serves to suggest that human nature has not fundamentally changed over the past two thousand years[106].

Inevitably, the fine detail of much of Sun Tzu's writing does not survive the passage of time and thus many of his wisdoms have been lost in their translation from the ancient Chinese characters in which they were painted. In an effort to make Sun Tzu more accessible and relevant to our contemporary Western culture, we need to reinterpret his ideas within a more modern context rather than as originally applied to the battlefields of ancient China.

"The wise warrior avoids combat." – Sun Tzu

---

[106] 'The Art of War' by Sun Tzu was widely believed to have been written in the 5th Century B.C.

The importance of strategy in achieving your goals

In his writing Sun Tzu goes to great lengths to explain the importance of visualisation and planning before undertaking any venture, including open warfare. As in chess or for any substantial investment decision, it is important to spend time deliberating and considering all eventualities before making any decisive moves. The great general talks at length about studying the nature of the terrain and its potential avenues and pitfalls before choosing a potential route or battlefield. Taking advantage of suitable weather and any natural cover is considered a wise strategy, while exposing yourself to the volatility of the elements and the unknown is presented as the road to ruin. Sun Tzu goes to great lengths to suggest that we should familiarise ourselves with all aspects of any endeavour, whether this be investing on the stock market or undertaking a research expedition. In fact, he goes further, arguing that those who act without due consideration or planning are destined to fail, while those who proceed only after meticulous preparation are guaranteed to succeed.

'The best way to hide something is if nobody knows of its existence.'

As we have discussed previously, if information is power, then misinformation presents us with a powerful defensive shield. Always seek to create a fog of uncertainty as to your true intentions and thus, if someone has an unhealthy interest in your affairs, then you should only offer them some confusing or suggestive bait that distracts them from the true scent of your trail. Any successful commercial or business activity involves a degree of secrecy and confidentiality. After all, you would not leave copies of your personal bank statements or an unlocked mobile phone on your coffee table for your friends and family to peruse, let alone for the scrutiny of strangers. If this is true for your closest friends and family, then why would it be inappropriate for you to be guarded over information relating to your plans, movements and ideas when dealing with other acquaintances? *Remember that there is no secret more secure than one which nobody is aware of, and no treasure safer than one whose existence is unknown.*

Achieving peace of mind and prosperity depends upon our ability to ensure that those who harbour ill will towards us cannot fathom our plans or desires. Sun Tzu cautions that we should always conceal our true intentions and hide any underlying fortitude or frailty in our position. This disorientates our opponents, giving the impression that we are in a position of strength when we are really in a state of weakness, or are at a loss when in fact we are ready to make our move. If we are about to realise our goals, we should seek to give the impression that we are still only within the planning stage and, if we are well aware of a glaring opportunity, then we should feign ignorance. Sun Tzu perceived arrogance and vanity to be fundamental flaws of character and urged that we should understate not only the strength of our position, but also the extent of our knowledge and abilities.[107] This is intended to lower the guard of potential rivals and thus make our approach to any given objective less fraught. The ancient general also advocated designing strategies which possess formless flexibility or, in other words, no fixed structure or agenda. This enables us to be adaptable and responsive to all eventualities.

'In preparing for battle, I have always found that plans are useless, but planning is indispensable.' - Dwight D. Eisenhower[108]

Sun Tzu advises us not to repeat a strategy with which we have previously been successful. This is not only because the prevailing factors may have changed to our disadvantage, but also because our competitors may have seized upon the secret of our earlier success. Specifically, he cautions that we should, *'not repeat the tactics which have gained you one victory, but let your methods be regulated by the infinite variety of circumstances.'* Sun Tzu employs a musical

---

[107] Those who court publicity often demand tribute and fanfare for their 'achievements' and triumphs, even when they are in fact hollow. Both Ramesses II and Napoleon returned triumphantly from campaigns in the Middle-East, proclaiming victory, when in actual fact they had suffered ignominious defeats.
[108] 34th U.S. President and celebrated WWII U.S. Army General

metaphor to make his point. Just as an infinite number of melodies can be created from a small number of notes, so we can create countless effective strategies from only a handful of guiding elements and principles.

The undefeated general advocated that we should always do the unexpected after we have already openly discussed the obvious - as our rivals and adversaries (both known and unsuspected) will take the bait - leaving us with a clear and unhindered path towards our objective.

Never let anyone convince you that there is no alternative to the course of action that is laid out by them – there is always an alternative option if your mind is receptive to other possibilities. Many great commanders achieved astounding victories by doing the unexpected. General Wolfe conquered Quebec by sending a force of nine thousand men and two cannons to scale a 200 metre cliff that towered above the St. Lawrence river - a cliff face that was considered unclimbable by the occupying French forces who were taken completely by surprise. The army of Napoleon emerged unexpectedly from the misty marshes of Austerlitz to gain victory over an enemy who dominated the high ground; while Genghis Khan once conquered a walled city by sending his forces across an impenetrable desert.

It is often the case that innovation succeeds where the recycling of old ideas fails. The creation of a search algorithm which could mine all the websites of the Internet for information was once simply inconceivable; yet this ingenious approach made Google one of the most successful companies of the 21st Century. The idea of broadcasting very short messages to a fixed fan base led to Twitter becoming a social phenomenon, while the 'self-destructing' messages of SnapChat certainly held the attention of a more youthful generation. Whether we consider the reinvention of the vacuum cleaner or the evolution of the electric car, a creative mind which is in tune with the emerging wave front of society can make even the most unexpected idea powerful.

Despite his prowess as a warlord, Sun Tzu went to great lengths to emphasise that peace should always be regarded as the highest objective, cautioning against resorting to conflict, except as a last resort. His quotes on this principle are numerous, from never attacking a retreating enemy, to always offering an opponent a dignified exit from the battlefield. Sun Tzu regarded achieving one's objectives without actual conflict as being the highest measure of success, as this avoids an inevitable loss of time, energy and resources. He wisely advises us that, *'the greatest victory is that which requires no battle.'*

The creation of opportunity

As a master strategist Sun Tzu understood that *'fortune favours the prepared mind.'* He also believed that opportunity is what we harvest from our enterprise. In other terms, not only do we have to be able to recognise and seize opportunity when it arises, but we also have to sow the seeds of our good fortune and wait to reap our rewards with a prepared mind. For instance, meeting the right person or business partner is not blind luck, but a culmination of the preparation of self and ensuring that we are in the right place at the right time. Good fortune may visit all of us from time to time, but some people are evidently luckier than others, simply because they seek and create opportunities and are ready to seize it when it presents itself.

With respect to being grounded in our ambitions, Sun Tzu advises that we should not seek to achieve the impossible, or to take on giants on their own ground, but rather to take advantage of those opportunities which are more readily harvested. Major objectives can however be realised through a series of smaller steps, as only the unwise rush in to seize an opportunity which would require substantial time and resources to consolidate[109]. To succeed in any major undertaking, we should master our skills and refine our strategy to the point where we are able to take a series of smaller objectives in view of attaining our greater goal. *For instance,* presenting a major exhibition of art work would normally only be accomplished after producing a series of notable pieces and by turning the heads of one or two influential collectors or dealers. Simply turning up at the door of a prestigious art gallery with a portfolio under one arm is unlikely to prove a fruitful strategy. In a similar vein, attempting to gain a share of the mobile phone sector by coding an entirely new operating system is almost certainly destined to

---

[109] For example, the invasion of Iraq by UK and US forces in 2003, which took only 6 weeks to achieve, but resulted in 8 years of occupation and insurgencies before the eventual withdrawal of forces in 2011.

fail, although it could become a reality, in time, if an entrepreneur entered the market by releasing one useful app at a time...

Sun Tzu reflects a great deal on the subject of opportunity, which he evidently went to great lengths to cultivate. He viewed opportunity as arising through three distinct channels, specifically *events*, *trends*, and *conditions*. To seize an opportunity arising through a train of events, one requires sharpness of mind or *'responsivity'*; to take advantage of good fortune deriving from a pattern or trend, one requires the wisdom of foresight; although when opportunity emerges from sudden and dramatic changes in the prevailing conditions *(e.g. a stock market crash or the outbreak of war)*, then bold action is required to grasp the initiative. To quote the words of the great general, *'in the midst of chaos, there is also opportunity.'*

A fastidious planner, Sun Tzu advocated that we should visualise all potential outcomes and prepare for each in turn, arguing that the tactician who prevails is the one who makes many calculations before engaging in operations, while the one who heads out to the battlefield before considering all eventualities is destined to fail.

Much of Sun Tzu's wisdom has been overlooked, simply because it was phrased within a militaristic context, yet his principles may be applied to any enterprise or endeavour, explaining his enduring popularity. The general would certainly argue that we should seek to cultivate new markets and opportunities rather than to continue to plough well-worn ground *(which has, by definition, been long established and exploited)*. Sun Tzu preached the importance of innovation in our approach to cultivate fresh fortunes.

The importance of timing & momentum

Now that we have refined our methods, improved our efficiency and prepared our minds for opportunity, we need to realise the importance of timing and momentum in attaining and securing our objectives. Good fortune is often a short-lived phenomenon and, although success can be contagious, it is of fundamental importance that we move at the right time to seize an opportunity and, once realised, ensure that our momentum does not grind to a halt.

On timing

Sun Tzu recognised that speed and timing are essential in securing any objective. When you are hunting for such an opportunity stay alert and prepared, pausing only when your goal has been achieved. As the master of strategy eloquently puts it, *'the quality of a decision is like the well-timed swoop of a falcon which enables it to strike and capture its prey within a single blow.'*

When the long-awaited opportunity finally arises you should already be prepared for action. When you do make your move, do so decisively, keeping your key objectives in mind. Attain only your pre-defined goals, and do not overstretch yourself or your resources. When a goal is achieved, seek to consolidate your gains and to make the most of your good fortune. Advance through a series of clearly visualised steps, and do not allow yourself to become intoxicated by the euphoria of an early success which may then cause you to overstep the mark. When you do this, you will quickly lose sight of your objectives and may overextend yourself to the point of becoming vulnerable in terms of your time and resources. *For example*, an early surge in book sales following a promotional tour or marketing campaign may be encouraging to an author, but it would not be wise to suddenly order stock in bulk in anticipation of future orders. Similarly, if an artist is able to sell her first set of photographs to a magazine or a fine art dealer, it would not be prudent to suddenly 'splash out' on a new camera or studio and make plans to leave her office job. It may be a good start, but first we have to *make success a habit*.

When it comes to the momentous decision to act, it should be an all-or-nothing commitment. If there is any reasonable doubt lingering within your mind, or an important unknown remains elusive, then it may be wiser to wait until the fog of uncertainty has cleared. If you make your move too soon, or without considering all the consequences and repercussions of taking your objective, you may find yourself with an unstable footing, unable to secure or consolidate your gains. This is a common error, especially in business, where an entrepreneur agrees to fulfil a large or difficult order in the hope that the necessary finance, suppliers or product will materialise to meet the specifications of the client. Remember that all the necessary elements have to be in place before you can say 'yes' to any major contract or financial commitment.

If you are approached by a client with a major opportunity, an honest response stating that you are unable to fulfil the order or to meet the client's specifications at that point in time will at least gain you their confidence. In due time, you may well find that you will be offered an opportunity that you can rise to the challenge of.

On momentum

There is a simple law of momentum in crossing the gain line and staying ahead of it. Remember that it **takes far more energy to put an object or plan into motion than it does to keep it in motion.**

Never undervalue what you have sacrificed so much to achieve and create. *Every day decide which steps, no matter how small, you are going to undertake in order to maintain your momentum.* Sometimes the smallest action, thought or realisation may be the key to the advancement of your goals. For instance, after many months of thought and reflection, it may suddenly occur to you one evening that your marketing plan lacks clarity and a focused market. There is a dawn of realisation that you have yet to fully explore the potential of local markets, and so you decide to jot down a few key words and phrases for an online search later that evening. This search yields dozens of potential local clients and also identifies several trade magazines which may yet provide an affordable opportunity to reach out to a national niche market for your product. You resolve to work out a budget and to call the magazines on Monday morning to negotiate some advertising space.

In terms of your approach towards your intended goal, Sun Tzu emphasizes the importance of flexibility and adaptability, again returning to the metaphor of water, as *'water shapes its course according to the nature of the ground over which it flows'*, just as successful entrepreneurs adapt their strategy to a continuously evolving market. He also places particular focus upon taking the least inhibited channel to reach the opportunity, thereby avoiding difficult terrain or obstacles, just as, *'flowing water avoids the heights and hastens to the lowlands.'* By adopting this approach, we can evade powerful adversaries and obstacles in seeking to exploit easier opportunities.

Sun Tzu also recognised that success is a 'snowball', in that momentum is attained through the successful application of an appropriate strategy and, if this is done, *'opportunities will multiply as they are realised.'* Again, returning to the theme of water, he explains how major obstacles may be overcome by the momentum of success, as *'when torrential water tosses boulders, it is through its momentum.'*

The Chinese sage has one further wisdom for us to reflect upon. A successful idea or strategy is readily replicated and, before long, we will find that our progress begins to grind to a halt. A successful idea, or *'meme'*[110], may be swiftly adopted and emulated, just as the discovery of a pristine new beach soon leads to its overpopulation. Thus innovation in our approach and strategy must be never ending, as even a famed artist may find that their work, once considered revolutionary, soon becomes conventional. As ever, Sun Tzu frames this wisdom within a few well-chosen words, *'therefore success is not repetitious, but adapts its form endlessly.'* The ultimate secret of success, as epitomised by Apple and David Bowie, derives from their ceaseless reinvention and innovation, as every fresh idea soon becomes history.

We shall leave the final words to Sun Tzu, *'A successful force has no constant formation, just as water has no constant shape - the ability to gain victory by changing and adapting according to the prevailing circumstances is otherwise called genius.'*

---

[110] 'An element of a culture, fashion or social behaviour which is passed from one individual to another by imitation because it is a good idea.' Attributed to Richard Dawkins in 'The Selfish Gene' 1976.

Chapter Eleven

Crossing the gain line

'There is no scarcity of opportunity to make a living at what you love - there's only scarcity of resolve to make it happen.' - Wayne Dyer[111]

Throughout this book we have discussed how the adoption of simple philosophies, behaviours and strategies enables us to make sense of a complex world and to move forward with a clearer vision. When we become lost, we have to pause to recover our bearings before we can continue on with our journey. Similarly, unless we can make rational sense of our lives and our place in the world, we will continue to make bad decisions and be unable to find our way to a desired destination.

However, it should be emphasised that this book is intended to serve as a philosophical compass rather than as a roadmap, as we all have a unique journey through life. It is hoped, whichever path you choose to take, that it will lead you to towards a more contented, prosperous and harmonious way of life.

As sentient beings, our perspective of the world is uniquely our own, and no one else should be able to dictate our place within it or the way in which we view it. Accept only that which you believe to be true, and reject that which you reason to be false or irrelevant. Absorb what is useful, adapting it to your purposes, and discard all those behaviours, distractions and devices which serve no rational or constructive purpose.

The primary intention of this guide is to open your mind to previously unexplored possibilities and to the realisation that you may, deep inside, be genuinely unhappy. The positive message

---

[111] American philosopher & author, 1940 - 2015

of this book is that it is never too late to pursue your own path towards self-fulfilment and happiness. Life is a series of moments which we collectively refer to as memories, and it is possible, even at the eleventh hour, to go to our final rest with a mind that is at peace and full of such happy moments. Even if you currently work long hours, this guide has sought to explain how you can still recover the necessary time to kindle a new passion or hobby. Irrespective of your present workload, *it is still realistic* to consider starting a new career or business within your reclaimed hours and to cultivate this venture until the day finally comes when you are able to make it your primary preoccupation.

A balance between life and work is attainable, and we all have the ability to find happiness without feeling a sense of 'guilt' for *'abandoning our obligations'*. This is however not always an easy journey, as we must first be prepared to confront the possibility that we are, despite our outward pretences and cheerfulness, essentially dispirited, and come to terms with the realisation that many of our existing behaviours and beliefs have no rational or ideological foundation. Once we have accepted these home truths, then the path towards fulfilment and happiness simply becomes a matter of visualising our goals.

In essence this book is very much a journey of introspection - a re-evaluation of the core values we have assimilated through the course of our formative education and social enculturation. It is only by releasing ourselves from the psychological prison of unreasonable expectations and fruitless burdens that we can relax our inner mind and regain the ability to see the world as a place of wonderment and opportunity. Imagination is a wonderful tool, but it is of little value to us if our dreams are not turned into deeds, culminating in the creation of something that is of genuine substance and value.

Hopefully, if you have read through this book in its intended sequence, then you will have adopted the essential 'tool kit' that explains how you can quickly liberate a great deal of wasted time and energy. The emancipated time will permit you to regain your verve and vitality and to refocus your mind upon those goals which inspire you and serve to make life more rewarding.

Once we have learned to harness the power of our subconscious minds to visualise and explore the myriad possibilities that are actually available to us, then our creative consciousness will be unleased. We all possess the power to recreate ourselves in our desired image rather than to be forged by the will of others.

It should be our goal to realise our full potential within all the dimensions of our lives, for this is the key to self-fulfilment and contentment.

Epilogue

The genesis of the book

'Have no way as way, and no limitation as limitation.'

Having endured an expensive, though not especially privileged education, the author left school and headed straight to university (owing to paternal pressure to follow a long family line of medical doctors). Having been convinced at school that he had precious little artistic aptitude, was essentially a mathematical dullard, and possessed only a modest scientific ability, he quickly found that the relentless pace of medical school and the conservative nature of his student contemporaries left him very much the odd man out. An innate curiosity, coupled with an inability to memorise reams of random facts, did not suit the requirements of a modern medical school and he soon left to pursue a nascent fascination for the chemistry of life.

It was while studying at a provincial university that the author finally found his feet, running a successful security company during the evenings and weekends[112]. As he began to explore his potential, he developed an active interest in natural bodybuilding and the martial arts, and soon realised that it was possible to achieve almost anything one put one's mind to. After a relatively adventurous few years he graduated and, to his surprise, found himself accepted for a PhD studentship in Biophysics at the University of Cambridge, adapting swiftly to the pressures of research and discovery - no mean feat for a young man who was perceived to have 'no mathematical ability'.

Whilst at Cambridge he dabbled in college politics and, after realising that this was not a happy hunting ground, hurriedly left the United Kingdom for New York with his PhD and newly acquired skill set. For the next ten years the world of research carried him across the length

---

[112] These adventures are recounted in the book 'Moon Waxing' by the same author.

and breadth of Europe and America, culminating in an evanescent position as a laboratory head. However, the joint position between laboratories in Germany and Los Angeles fell through within six months and, before long, he realised that he had become a former neuroscientist, despite making over thirty discoveries within a decade.

This sudden professional vacuum necessitated the acquisition of a new skill set, as electrophysiology and molecular biology are not generally in great demand on main street. Entirely unaided and unfunded, he taught himself web programming, professional photography, business and economics.

In the twelve years since his departure from the insular world of research, the author has become a well-known photographer, started a fashion model agency, and published no fewer than five books – all beyond the confines of his day job as the director of an editing company in London.

It can be done...

Crossing the gain line

Synopsis

In the modern world many of us find that we have little time for ourselves or what makes us happy. We sleep for some eight hours a night, spend two hours a day commuting, another two preparing and eating food, and at least two more dealing with countless messages and other daily chores. This leaves us with only ten hours a day, which, for most of us, is taken up by what we do for a living...

Unsurprisingly, many of us find it impossible to move forward with our lives or to achieve our dreams and aspirations. The good news is that it is never too late to find a balance between work and play, to start a business of your own, or to cultivate a new passion or hobby. **Crossing the Gain Line** explains how we can, by making a few simple adjustments to our approach and guiding philosophy, reclaim lost time and begin our journey towards self-fulfilment and happiness. Read this book before it is too late...

17065826R00079

Printed in Poland
by Amazon Fulfillment
Poland Sp. z o.o., Wrocław